# SUCH
# IS
# LIFE

SARAH BERGSTEIN

# SUCH
# IS
# LIFE

29 Life Revelations from a
30-Year-Old Dreamer

SUCH IS LIFE

Such is Life: 29 Life Revelations from a 30-Year-Old-Dreamer

Sarah Bergstein
sarahbergstein.com
info@sarahbergstein.com

Front and Back Cover Design by Sarah and Outward Bound Collective
facebook.com/OBCollective

Cover and Author Photos by Bernie Kale

Interior design by Sarah Bergstein and Chris Hoyler

All "Notes from the Universe" © Mike Dooley, TUT.com

ISBN 978-0-9993456-0-3

For more:

Visit: sarahbergstein.com
Email: info@sarahbergstein.com
Connect: facebook.com/sarahbergstein, instagram.com/sarahbergstein, twitter.com/sarah_bergstein

*To all the young girls out there making their way in the world:*

*I see you.*

*I get you.*

*And I absolutely know what it's like.*

*No, it's not easy.*

*Life, I mean.*

*But I can promise you it'll all be worth it.*

*Just keep going.*

*You'll see.*

---

*To Josh, Jackie, and Mitch:*

*I love you guys endlessly. Bergsteins always stick together.*

# Contents

# Author's Note

**rev-e-la-tion**
*noun*

1. a surprising and previously unknown fact, especially one that is made known in a dramatic way
   *"revelations about his personal life"*
   synonyms: disclosure, surprising fact, announcement, report
2. the divine or supernatural disclosure to humans of something relating to human existence or the world
   *"an attempt to reconcile Darwinian theories with biblical revelation"*

Thank you so much for your interest in my very first book! I wanted to take a minute and tell you about a few key things throughout so their significance doesn't go unnoticed.

First: The cover, shot by Bernie Kale of Outward Bound Collective. We chose this cover because it's the purest and most simple concept for how to enjoy this book. Each of the 29 revelations are relatively short, digestible stories. They can be read and enjoyed each on their own, one at time. Grab a cup of coffee and read one a day, or make the whole pot and get ready for quite a journey. However you choose to enjoy this book—with whatever your beverage of choice—I'd love for you to show me!

Tag me in your photos with your copy—reading the book, enjoying it with coffee, on the go, on vacation, or in whatever way is most fitting for you. Don't forget to tag me @sarahbergstein and use the hashtag #suchislifethebook so I'm certain to see it. I can't wait to see and share your photos, so keep them coming!

Second: You'll find at the beginning of every chapter, not a quote, but a message from "The Universe." I've subscribed to Mike Dooley of TUT's "Notes from the Universe" (© Mike Dooley, TUT.com) daily emails since early 2013 and have read them every single day since. It's the first thing I do when I wake up in the morning to begin my day. I even have a dedicated folder in my email where I save all of the best ones, and felt this was a perfect way to share my favorites from over the years with you.

Head to TUT.com to subscribe and get your "Notes from the Universe" delivered to your inbox daily. I hope you love them just as much as I have!

Third: This book is a culmination of my life up to this point. In it, I share stories that are very personal to me about people and situations that have had great impact on my life. Please note that every chapter was written with extreme care and painstaking detail to get the stories right. I love this advice by Anne Lamott: "You own everything that happened to you. Tell your stories. If people wanted you to write warmly about them, they should've behaved better."

But regardless of how much I love her words, some names and minor details have been changed to protect individuals who'd asked for my consideration of their privacy, to which I absolutely granted in any instance. Those details do not, in any way, alter the truth of this work.

Finally, thank you again. Writing this book has been cleansing for my soul and it is a true gift to be able to share it. I ask that if you enjoy *Such is Life* and my stories, could you be so kind and be sure to leave a review on Amazon when you're done, and tell your family and friends about it?

Each time this book is reviewed and shared it has one more chance to end up in the hands of someone who may take away something very important, as I have from so many books that've been recommended to me over the years.

One more time…thank you. I feel like I can't say it enough. I'm thrilled to have the opportunity to spend this moment in time together with you and I look forward to hearing from you if you'd like to connect with me in any of the following ways below.

Happy reading!
Sarah

P.S. Would you like a free *Such is Life* "29 Revelations" printable that you can hang in a special place for ongoing motivation and inspiration? Head to sarahbergstein.com/book to get your hands on your very own free printable!

Connect with me:
Email: info@sarahbergstein.com
Facebook: Sarah Bergstein or facebook.com/sarahbergstein
Instagram: @sarahbergstein or instagram.com/sarahbergstein
Twitter: @sarah_bergstein or twitter.com/sarah_bergstein
Website: sarahbergstein.com

# Introduction

My mom always says, "Such is life."

It didn't matter if something went perfectly right, terribly wrong, or just differently than expected. She'd shrug her shoulders and say, "Hmph. Such is life."

As teens, my sister and I always thought it was funny. Jaclyn is two years younger than me and that proximity in age has allowed us to have a special relationship at every phase of our lives.

"SUCH IS LIFE!" we'd echo together and laugh at my mom's quirky saying.

Then while in college together, we adopted our mom's saying and used it in every scenario we felt that mom would.

There've been so many good times in my life up to this point. There've been plenty of really crappy times, too.

In my early 20s, my mom said over the phone to me, "You should really write a book about all of your experiences and the things you've been through, so that girls your age who may be struggling won't feel so alone."

I loved the idea and I had plenty to write about.

So one day I opened a Word document on my laptop and created a title page.

"Such is Life," I called it.

I made lists and outlines and tried to capture everything I'd want to include in that book. Then I wrote a few things down here and there as draft chapters, but never got too far.

The longer I thought about this book being a reality, the more I talked myself out of it.

*I'm too young.*

*I have no audience.*

*Who the heck would want to read about my life, anyway?* were the things I said to myself.

After doing research about how to get a book deal with an agent and a publisher and how much it could cost—both in time, but mainly in money I didn't have—it seemed like maybe it wasn't in the cards for me.

I also wasn't totally comfortable with sharing my story in those days.

In your early 20s, turning 30 seems like forever away.

So I put the book idea aside and told myself that my goal could be to publish a book before I turned 30 years old.

I reasoned that it would give me plenty of time to figure things out along the way.

Fast forward to April 2017. It's six months before my 30th birthday and still I have no book, no agent, no book deal, and a relatively small social media following as an audience.

*Such is life.* Right?

But I've learned since I first created that book title page almost a decade ago, that just because the goal seems too hard, too big, or too far away, doesn't mean you should change the goal.

Instead, you should change your methods and do everything in your power to reach it.

*This is my story,* I thought, *and I could absolutely tell it in under six months.*

And then the light came on. I could still reach my goal.

So I set out on this journey of sharing the story of my life so far.

It happens to be perfect timing.

As I'm writing this, I'm in a period of transition from my incredible career as an Air Force public affairs officer to my dream career of being an entrepreneur.

Because this year has been a time of so much change for me, I've spent a lot of time thinking about the things that make me who I am, where I come from, and how I've made it this far.

I've thought a lot about all the things I've learned, the struggles I've endured, and the hardships I've worked through.

I've thought about the lessons I've learned about life—everything from love to fear to success to struggle to leadership and how to navigate every kind of relationship.

I've thought about how many times I've failed and then pulled through, the number of times my family has struggled and then succeeded, and how many people I know, all the books I've read, and stories I've heard about success through adversity.

The revelations—or lessons—you'll read in the pages that follow, are ones that I've personally picked up along the way.

And the stories I share are my real-world examples of learning these lessons, be it from my family, relationships, friends, my career, or my life experiences.

Conveniently, there are 29 lessons.

To make things even more fun, I've published and released this book on October 16, 2017.

The very date of my 30th birthday.

*Goal accomplished.*

These are the stories that have shaped who I am today, from the people and situations who've touched my life in so many different ways.

Now of course, many of the situations and stories from that original outline are included in this book, but a lot has happened in the years since that first draft, and I'll share with you those stories, too.

As I begin a new chapter of my life, this season of change has made me think a lot about what I'm capable of.

In opening up and sharing so much of my life, I hope I remind you to look within and reflect on who you are, where you've been, and the stories that make you who you are, so that you're consciously aware of all that's possible for you, too.

Whoever you are, wherever you are in the world, whenever you're reading this, at whatever point you're at in your life, and no matter what you're going through, know that you're not alone, that everything is temporary, and that you have the power to change your mind, change your day, and change your life at any time.

Because as my mom always says, "It begins with you and ends with you."

I've got 30 years of life to fill you in on.

So let's begin.

# The
# 29 Revelations

# Revelation 1:

## *One day at a time.*

I went to my first Alcoholics Anonymous meeting when I was seven years old.

My mom was never a raging drunk, but we come from a healthy line of alcoholics, and she found herself in a place that was concerning to her.

So I tagged along with her to meetings from the beginning, the same way I tagged along on every trip to the grocery store, every Kmart run, and every stop by the gas station for her pack of cigarettes.

To you, I imagine that sounds insane, and perhaps like a poor parenting choice. But it's my story.

Such is life.

For as far back as I have memories, my mom has been my hero.

I love absolutely everything about her, even the things that drive me totally freaking mad.

She's my first example, and thus my definition, of true love.

She's wonderful and sweet and impatient and flawed and I can't get enough.

Hands down, she's one of the coolest human beings you'll ever meet.

And so I begged her to take me with her to AA meetings, just for another hour to spend with her.

Maybe my story is different from other kids who've lived with alcoholic parents, because I never saw my mom drunk once in my whole life.

She was the kind of drinker that left me and my three siblings, all under the age of nine, at home with my dad on a Friday night so she could cut loose at the bar.

Then she'd stumble in during the dead of night, long after my dad had already put us all to bed and gone to sleep, too.

If you told me as a kid my mom had a drinking problem, I'd say you had the wrong mommy.

But I think we all get to a place in life where enough is enough, when it comes to any obsessive habit or lack of one at all—like smoking too much or not exercising enough.

In my mom's case, enough was enough of the Fridays at the bar coming home wasted long after her family was asleep.

On August 11, 1994, she found her way to "The Rooms" of AA and into a life of recovery.

As a kid, I hung out in the playrooms of the churches where the meetings were held, either by myself or with the kids of other recovering alcoholics. When I'd hear the chairs shifting, I'd rush back to the room to hold my mom and another person's hand as everyone circled up for the "Our Father" and "Serenity Prayer" at the end of the meeting. I recited every word loud and proud.

"Keep coming back. It works if you work it...and you're worth it, so work it!" I'd cheer.

In my teens, I started sitting with my mom through the hour-long meeting, listening to stories of suffering men and women sharing their heart and working to save themselves from a disease that, it seems, tears apart more families than kills people.

The one thing I learned early on is that every single person had problems, and all of them were working on bettering their lives. Because none of them could do it alone, they found themselves in The Rooms, together.

I didn't hear my mom share frequently, but when I did, my palms would sweat like crazy.

As her daughter, I was scared to hear her share pieces of her life that didn't fit my image of her.

On the other hand, I couldn't have been prouder. I even sat a little taller in my chair.

While she shared, I'd look first at her, then around the room, and you could plainly see that people were just as mesmerized by her as I'd always been.

There's a feeling about being my mother's daughter. It's like a vibration, and even now while I'm typing this, my palms are sweating.

When we'd step out of the car and into the circle of recovering alcoholics gathered in a church parking lot smoking cigarettes, drinking coffee, hugging, and saying hello—in that space my mom was the coolest person I'd ever known.

People flocked to her. Their faces lit up when they saw her. They threw their arms around her, kissed her, and loved on her. It was common that someone would come up to her and say, "You're Sharon, right?" And because I was her daughter, I got all that same love, too.

She has so many friends in the Program and all of these people became like family to me. They supported me through middle school, high school, and into college, and still cheer me on to this day.

From the very beginning I loved going to meetings.

I asked to go every weekend, and she always said yes.

I loved getting in our old heap-of-junk van and driving to Dunkin' Donuts, where she ordered a, "Large with cream and two Sweet'n Low," the same coffee she still orders to this day.

I loved pulling up to the parking lot of the various churches and seeing familiar faces waiting to love on us.

I loved the way the rooms smelled like bitter coffee and faint cigarette smoke and old Bibles.

And I loved the way I felt after leaving a meeting.

To this day, I haven't asked my mom why she let me go with her to meetings.

Why would she expose me to a room full of drunks when I was just a kid?

It doesn't matter the reason. And if I asked her, she'd probably say she never thought twice about it. Or that she'd said yes simply because I asked.

The people I've met in The Rooms of AA are some of the kindest, gentlest, smartest, most hardworking, incredibly strong people I've ever known. They come from all walks of life, they all have their own story, and every single one of them has fought like a gladiator to turn their lives around.

Those are my kind of people.

I say that everything I've learned in life is from my mom and dad and a bunch of drunks.

In the 23 years of my mom's sobriety, I've become the person I am today. My life is infinitely better for all the little moments where her one decision to stop drinking made all the difference for me.

This unique experience from early in my life has shaped so many of the opportunities I've had and the directions I've taken up to this point.

I am absolutely my mother's daughter, and I'd bet a lot of money that phrase has never been used so proudly. If by some amazing miracle I become even just half the woman she is, then I am certain to live an incredibly full and amazing life.

Each year in high school I had the opportunity to present to my mom her AA anniversary coin.

We'd go to the meeting to celebrate all the anniversaries taking place that month and would clap and cheer and love on the people celebrating 10 years, one day, 10 months, 15 years, 35 years of sobriety.

Talk about a good feeling.

Then the time would come for me to give my mom her coin. As we stood at the front of the room, each year I'd say something to the tune of, "Thank you to all the parents in the room who've chosen, fought for, and persisted in their sobriety. I'm the daughter of a mother who lives one day at a time, and her sobriety has created more opportunities for me than I ever would've had, had she continued down that same path. Thank you to every single mom and dad in this room who also lives one day at a time. We, as your children, have a life today because of your commitment to recovery."

In the Program they say, "If you have decided you want what we have and are willing to go to any length to get it—then you are ready to take certain steps."

I decided I always wanted that *thing* my mom has. Her wisdom, experience, and her love of life, and of other people.

Her ability to take life one day at a time.

Admittedly, this way of living is still extremely hard for me.

Of all the lessons I've learned, this one eludes me.

One day at a time is the only way to live. It's that simple.

It's just not easy.

I personally struggle getting caught up in my past and thinking too often about the future—not fully living in the day.

It may seem like there's no cost to living this way, in a manner where you live in the past or future instead of the present. But the price to pay, as I've found, is true happiness.

I've never met a person who doesn't want to be truly and fully happy.

So I love the saying, "There is no path to happiness. Happiness *is* the path."

And while I've tried to walk that path my way so many times, I'm learning the only way to walk it happily is one day at a time.

If this concept eludes you, too, you're not alone.

Taking life one day at a time is not easier. In fact, it's much harder.

That's why it's worth it.

When you can learn from and let go of the past, and have hope and faith in the future—without letting either or both control you—you're free to live for today.

Twenty-three years ago my mom made the decision to live her life one day at a time. It wasn't going to be easy. She had no idea of everything she had to let go of, and all that her future could become.

But she just kept going, one day at a time.

As am I.

Keep coming back. It works if you work it...and you're worth it, so work it.

# Revelation 2:

## *Not all blessings come in good things.*

If it weren't for your challenges, how would you ever
know that there are things you still misunderstand?
You wouldn't. Bless them. Embrace them. Give thanks.

Tallyho, ho, ho,
The Universe

My phone rang. It was mom. She asked me if I was sitting down.

"We're losing the house, your father and I are getting a divorce, and your dad lost his job."

I took a seat and looked around my bedroom. I'd just finished unpacking all of my things and spent hours perfectly hanging up my posters, pictures, and decorations. It was the summer of 2007 and my five girlfriends and I moved out of the dorms at Temple University in Philadelphia and into our very own newly-renovated rowhome just off campus for our sophomore year.

This was supposed to be my year...except now it wasn't.

I don't remember a single word of the rest of that conversation. But I'll piece together for you the aftermath.

I left that house and those girlfriends a few months later and moved everything back into my childhood bedroom in Allentown, Pennsylvania. I figured if we were going to lose the house I spent 19 years growing up in, I'd make the most of the time we had left in it.

That sounds sweet and sentimental, doesn't it?

Truth is, I had absolutely no idea what was going to happen next with my life.

Until that point, I thought I'd be doing what you're taught to do growing up: get good grades, get into a good college, get a good job, find someone and settle down, start a family...we all know the drill.

But then, it's as if all at once and piece by piece, what I thought were "givens" in my life now all seemed impossible.

*How the hell was I supposed to stay in school when my life around me was falling apart?*

Have you ever arrived at your destination in your car and wondered who drove the car? You're so consumed with something else that your brain drives on autopilot and you arrive at your destination, somehow unharmed.

That's what every aspect of my life felt like in the semester that followed.

I drove back and forth from Allentown to Philadelphia five days a week. Up at 4 a.m. for a 90-minute drive to school and then home in rush-hour traffic for homework and a few hours of sleep before doing it all over again.

On weekends, I worked the breakfast shift at Chris' Family Restaurant—the diner I'd worked at every Saturday and Sunday morning and during summer breaks since I was 15 years old.

The months that followed are mostly a giant hole in my memory. I can name only a few moments and memories here and there.

My boyfriend at the time, who was going to school in Colorado Springs, flew me out to Colorado for the weekend every few months, which felt like a getaway.

I went to class, partied with friends, explored the city, worked at the Diner, and held it together as best I knew how.

I look back at photos of myself during that time and I hardly recognize that girl. I was a fully-functioning person on the outside but terrified and depressed at almost every moment on the inside.

Then we moved out of our home the day after Christmas that year.

The day prior, there were no Christmas gifts. There wasn't a tree. We ate together at the dinner table that night in silence.

My two memories of our last dinner in our home are the sound of my mom crying, and the hope I held in my heart that our family would find a way to figure everything out—that we wouldn't fall apart through all the sadness.

Even though there were no gifts, I passed around dollar-store picture frames to my parents and my three siblings, each with three photos of our family.

The two outer photos were of the four of us kids. The photo in the middle was of our whole family when all four of us were really young. On the back of each frame I'd typed, printed, and taped something I'd written:

"You never see the hard times in the photographs, but they are what get you from one happy snapshot to the next. Wherever the road ahead may take you, remember always where it was you came from."

No matter what happened after we all stood up from that table for the very last time, I wanted each of us to be able to look at those photos and know that we'd always been a family.

So on December 26, 2007, my mom moved in with a friend from AA, who had a young daughter. Meanwhile, my dad moved into a small apartment—get this—exactly 3.1 miles down the exact same street my mom had just moved to. Just a 5K away.

My oldest brother, Josh, was a senior at Shippensburg University that year and graduated and went on to his first teaching job in Harrisburg, Pennsylvania. My younger twin brother and sister, Mitchell and Jaclyn, were seniors in high school.

To make space for the four of us, my sister had a room in the house my mom moved into. My younger brother and I both had a room at my dad's apartment. Josh didn't come home much during those years and honestly, I didn't blame him.

I've come to learn, both through the passing of time and because my mom always says it, that *not all blessings come in good things.*

And oftentimes, the blessing isn't revealed to us for quite some time.

It certainly wasn't in my or my family's case, so let's hold that thought while I tell you how things played out from here.

# Revelation 3:

## *There's no higher purpose than service.*

You are the one who was sent to make a difference, to be a bridge,
to light the way, by living the truths that have been revealed to you,
so that others might do the same. So now you know why you've
always seen the world so differently than others.

To help,
The Universe

"I'm not going to college," Mitchell said to my parents one
day after school. "It's a waste of my time and your money."

This declaration came in the months leading up to the
foreclosure, so it would've been easy to toss this onto the pile
of crap that my family had already been carrying that year.

*Oh great, now Mitch isn't going to college and will probably
end up a failure.*

Looking back, it's actually comical, and sweet, that Mitch
thought school would be paid for. My parents barely had the
money for groceries in those days, let alone to send either of
the twins to college.

Like most college students, Josh and I were already financing
our degrees with student loans and the expectation was that
Mitchell and Jaclyn would do the same. Jax had plans to join
me at Temple but Mitch had been completely noncommittal
and undecided up until that moment.

"I'm going into the Marine Corps," he then said. And in that moment, the youngest member of our family changed every single one of us.

I came home one afternoon in high school and noticed a DVD laying on the coffee table in the living room. "Peaceful Warrior," it was called, so I popped it into the DVD player and sat down on the edge of the coffee table to see what the movie was about.

I was the only one home that afternoon and I don't know what it was about the disc laying there on the table that made me stop whatever I was doing to watch it, but I did. And I was hooked.

I didn't find out until afterwards that it had been given to Mitch by a guy he worked with.

Rather than spoiling it I'll give you just a little peak, because the lessons in this movie (and in the book that inspired it, which I immediately read after) completely shook my world.

Dan Millman, the main character in the movie and the author of the book, meets a guy in his junior year at the University of California, Berkeley while training to become a world-champion gymnast.

This guy, whom Dan nicknames "Soc" (short for Socrates), is portrayed as this elusive and unpredictable man who teaches Dan "the way of the peaceful warrior."

These lessons come at a time when Dan needs them most, as he learns how to be not just a champion gymnast, but a stand-up man, too.

So one night Dan goes to meet Soc at his gas station and is mouthing off about his problems. The conversation goes something like this:

Soc: "You can live a whole lifetime without ever being awake."

Dan: "Hey Socrates, you know so much, how come you're working at a gas station?"

Soc: "This is a *service* station. We offer *service*. There's no higher purpose."

Dan: "Than pumping gas?"

Soc: "*Service. To others.*"

I saw this movie before there was ever a chance that Mitch would one day be a Marine. And aside from my grandfather who served 23 years in the Navy, there's been no one else on either side of my family who has volunteered and sacrificed to serve.

So it's not that Mitch felt the family pull or that he was following in the footsteps of those who came before us. My grandfather passed away a few months after I was born from gangrene in his legs, along with too many years of too much alcohol in his blood.

Mitchell's only ever heard those war stories from the second-hand perspective of our grandmother, which were followed by stories from my mom and her siblings about how our grandpa was a lousy dad in the aftermath of the Korean War.

But when the recruiter crossed paths with Mitch, it happened to have been the perfect timing for a young man with a seemingly bleak future to make something of himself.

At the time when Mitch enlisted, the Marine Corps' recruiting slogan was, "The few, the proud."

I'm sure you probably remember it.

Each time I'd see it on a billboard or poster, my mind flashed back to the scene with Soc and Dan in that gas station convenience store.

*Service to others. There's no higher purpose.*

I followed Mitch's journey proudly...and curiously. He started attending physical training sessions, studying for the military's standardized testing, and spending a lot of time at the recruiter's office in the strip mall down the street from our house. Before then, I never knew that recruiter's office even existed, let alone did I feel a call to serve myself. That came later, which we'll get to.

It was as if immediately Mitch became a Marine. You don't technically get that rite of passage and the honor to be called a Marine until you graduate from boot camp at Camp Lejeune in North Carolina. But in the months leading up to his departure for boot camp, he stood taller. He was focused. And his gaze was set on something in the future. It's not that he was a different person, but it was evident that his future was looking much brighter.

Mitch's military occupational specialty code, or MOS as they call it—his job—was a 0811 Field Artillery Cannoneer. In combat situations, Marines use different weapons to defend against and attack the enemy. One of the most effective weapons on the ground is the howitzer, a type of artillery that can double as a field gun or a cannon to produce indirect fire.

The howitzer needs more than one operator so there are several members of a field artillery howitzer battery, and one of the most important is the field artillery cannoneer—Mitch's job.

It's considered an entry-level position in the Marine Corps, but it's also one Marines can't go without.

So in August 2010 the call came for him to deploy.

Bravo Battery, 1st Battalion, 10th Marine Regiment, was headed to the Kajaki Dam, one of two major hydroelectric power dams of the Helmand province in southern Afghanistan—about 100 miles from Kandahar. He'd be there for a total of seven months, and we worried about him every single day that he was gone.

Mitchell served on active duty for four years, one of which he was deployed, the rest of the time spent at Twentynine Palms in California or Camp Lejeune.

While he came back to us safe and sound, some of his Marine brothers didn't, a very real and heavy reminder of the sacrifices paid by those who protect and defend this nation.

I owe a massive debt of gratitude to my baby brother. His courage changed my life for the better and inspired me to do more with my life, and for others, than I thought was possible for me at the time.

*Service to others. There's no higher purpose.*

# Revelation 4:

## *God never gives us more than we can handle.*

Every burden bears a gift, every challenge brings a treasure, and every setback hides a blessing. Is it just me, or does time and space sometimes seem far too good to be true?

Hallelujah,
The Universe

I mentioned this earlier, but as a refresher: In the summer before my sophomore year of college, I moved into a renovated rowhome just outside of Temple University's main campus. Now I want to tell you a different part of that story.

That summer, I was working as a waitress at TGI Fridays in Center City Philadelphia, so I moved into the house early with one other girl who also had a summer job.

People spent a lot of time out on their front stoops in the summer, and I met a lot of my new neighbors that way, including Miss Kathy, who lived just a few rowhomes up on the same street. I don't remember exactly when I met Miss Kathy, but I do remember that we instantly became close.

To me, it felt like the "old days" growing up in my suburban neighborhood, where you actually knew all your neighbors and kids played outside.

I had a pet rabbit at the time named Bruno, whom I'd take outside with me and let him hop around the stoop to get some fresh air. The neighborhood kids couldn't get over him. He was an all-gray, floppy-eared, big-as-a-cat rabbit.

I distinctly remember one of the little boys asking me, "Is that your dog?" These same kids would run their tiny hands through my long blonde hair, wondering if it was real and why it was so different from theirs.

My skin was different, my hair was different, and I had a cat-rabbit. These kids were fascinated, and I spent a lot of time sitting out on the stoop that summer being part of their world.

Soon after I'd met Miss Kathy, I ended up with a horrible case of poison sumac from volunteering at a city-wide cleanup event. From head to toe and everywhere in between I was covered in the stuff, and the doctor had me on steroids and doused in calamine lotion at all times.

Just before it got to its worst point I ran into Miss Kathy and showed her my battle wounds from working to do a good thing. She called me her "Boo Boo Baby," a name that stuck long after the poison healed, and a moment that solidified our friendship.

The summer passed, and with it came the news of losing the house, my dad losing his job, and the end of my parents' marriage.

I pressed on and acted like things were fine, as I told you, and I held onto my room in that house for as long as I could before moving back home and commuting to school each day.

By that time, I'd already been supporting myself for years because my parents raised us to get a job, finance a car, pay our own bills, and to have the responsibility to earn our own money.

So while I was attending school on student loans and had a part-time job and some money in the bank from years of working, the bills came faster than my waitressing tips, and I couldn't look to my parents for help.

Months had gone by since I'd seen Miss Kathy and I ran into her one day while walking to my car, which I usually parked near that house I moved out of.

She asked what'd happened to me and where I'd been, a question I got often during that time.

As we stood outside her house by her stoop on the street I used to live on, I told her about what was going on with my family and the current state of my life. I mentioned to her that I was thinking of dropping out of school to move back home and take more shifts at the Diner.

It was the first time I'd told someone that I was thinking of quitting school.

She looked up at the second-story windows in the front of her house and I followed her gaze.

She pointed to the windows, "You see that room right there?" she asked. "That room is empty, nobody lives in this house but me. I want you to bring your things. I want you to have a place to stay in my home. And I want you to stay in school."

And so that's what I did.

When I close my eyes I can still feel what it was like to live in Miss Kathy's house. I remember the smells, the mood of the lighting, and the setup of each room.

When you walked in the door you felt an overwhelming sense of peace.

She was a bit of a hoarder, so the house was packed with things. Not in a way that felt stressful, but in a way that felt like she held onto the things she loved dearly, and the reasons those things were brought into her life.

Pieces of paper were taped to the walls throughout the house that had Bible verses on them, and in the living room downstairs there was an old multi-CD stereo that was kept on just about all the time. The volume was turned down low, but speakers were wired to every room in the house, so that the subtle sound of gospel music played throughout the day. When you were silent or the house was quiet, you would hear it.

There was no working shower in the house and the bathtub faucet dripped cold water, so I learned to pack a shower bag and walk to the campus fitness center down the street in the freezing cold of winter to take a shower each day.

At night when the house got really cold, Miss Kathy would turn on the oven and keep it propped open to allow the heat to work its way into the living room from the kitchen. Sometimes we'd stand in front of it together to warm our hands, but most often we sat together in the living room at the end of each day and talked about everything under the sun.

I slept in several layers of clothes under a big pile of blankets each night and because I had Bruno there with me, I kept his cage mostly covered in a blanket to keep him warm, too.

I came and went to and from the house during the week for class, and on the weekends I'd load Bruno into the car and take him home so that I could work at the Diner.

One weekend when I got back to Philadelphia from working, Miss Kathy told me she was losing her home to foreclosure.

It felt like a bad dream or a sick joke.

While I was sad for her, I was right in the middle of the horrible experience with my family, so at the time I was only really thinking about what would happen to me, now that I'd had this new routine with school and work, and her house as my home.

She told me she'd be moving just one street over to live with her brother and his girlfriend and her baby, in the house she grew up in—her mom's house.

She said there was one spare room and that I could share it with her.

And that's what I did.

I'm not exactly sure what happened with all the stuff in Miss Kathy's house. I wasn't there the weekend all of it was moved.

But when I moved into our new shared bedroom I'd downsized my things to a few drawers of clothes, Bruno, and the things I needed for school. She had only a few things herself.

I never spent time in any other room of the house, except the bathroom (where there was a working shower). When I was there, I was sitting on my bed either doing homework or getting ready to sleep. Any other time of day was spent at class, working out of a coffee shop or at the student center on campus, or in my hometown working at the Diner.

While I wasn't there often, when Miss Kathy and I were home together in our bedroom, I loved every minute we spent together.

We'd sit on our beds and she'd pray out loud to God for me and my family each night while she braided her hair before bed. She knew my whole family by their names, and prayed that every single one of us would find peace and strength during that hard time.

We'd gotten to know so much about each other's lives, experiences, families, and our hopes for our futures.

And I'll never forget this story she told me.

Back when she was my age she'd recently gotten a job and moved into her first apartment. And the place was less than stellar. It was old and run down and not very safe, but it was her own. When it rained, the ceiling leaked in multiple places.

And so what did she do?

She set up a few makeshift buckets and grabbed a mop. As the rain would fall she'd work tirelessly to keep her place dry, all the while cheering out loud, "Thank you Jesus for this house. Thank you Jesus for this mop. Thank you Jesus for these buckets. Thank you Jesus for this rain."

While there's really no way to pinpoint just how incredible of a person Miss Kathy is, that very story says so much about her character. She's forever changed me.

I wondered if it was possible for me to be thankful for the "rain" in my life.

The part of this story that I hate is that Miss Kathy hasn't been in my life for almost 10 years.

One weekend after being at home working at the Diner, I came back to the house, climbed the stairs with Bruno, and got to our bedroom where everything from her side of the room was gone.

Her brother told me she'd decided to move to Texas to live with her daughter and, while I like to tell myself she must've had her reasons, she didn't say goodbye to me.

Her brother and his girlfriend let me stay in their house even though Miss Kathy had left, and I continued to live there for a few months before I'd saved enough money and was able to get a place on my own.

I never heard from her again after she moved, but to this day, I've kept her old number in my phone. I still call the number each year at Christmas, even though I know it won't ring through to her.

It sounds absolutely insane, but I never learned her full name outside of what I called her, Miss Kathy. And while even to me that does seem totally crazy now not to have known, at the time, when I was in survival mode, it just didn't matter.

I've tried so many different ways to reach her, or even her brother and his girlfriend, but I've never been able to find her.

I've often thought that she was an angel who came into my life at a time when I needed it most, and when she went on her way, it was because it was time for me to make the choice to move forward with my own life.

And so that's what I did.

During that time I learned, like my mom always says, *God never gives us more than we can handle.*

It's true.

Even when things seem to be the absolute worst that it could ever be, it eventually gets better. There is calm after the storm. There is a rainbow after the rain, and pain—while it may linger forever—is never as devastating as it may feel in the moment.

God never gave Miss Kathy more than she could handle.

Or me either.

Or even you.

# Revelation 5:

## *The rest of your life is a long time.*

In all battles of the heart over the mind, go with your heart.
Because, truly, it's a lot easier for your mind to catch up with
your heart, than for your heart to catch up with your mind.
A whole lot.

Tallyho,
The Universe

I'd been standing in front of the mirror for several minutes
repeating these sayings over and over again:

"I am nothing without Jacque."

"My life means nothing if I don't have him."

"I have nothing else if I don't have Jacque."

"Jacque is my whole world and everything revolves around
him."

"Mom, c'mon, this is really stupid," I said.

"That's the point, Sarah," she said. "This is really stupid.
You're a beautiful girl with your whole life ahead of you.
You're about to go to college and begin your future. I know
you're sad, but you will be ok without Jacque."

She was right. She was typically right about these kinds of
things. And in this instance, I knew she was right.

But it wasn't until my mom made me stand in front of that mirror in my bedroom, and recite those phrases over and over and over again, until it drove me to thinking about how stupid it really was to spend any more time being sad about having the chance to love someone so fully at such a young age, even if it didn't last forever.

Jacque and I dated for three years in high school. He'd graduated the year before and stayed in the area for community college. During my senior year, as I was applying to and visiting colleges and things were about to change for us, our relationship didn't survive the pressure.

"The rest of your life is a long time, Sarah," my mom assured me through what seemed like endless tears.

It makes me think of my favorite Cristina Yang line.

Perhaps this is a spoiler alert, but in the Season 10 finale of "Grey's Anatomy," she and Meredith get done dancing it out for one last time before Cristina leaves Seattle Grace Hospital to run cardiothoracic surgery at her own hospital in Switzerland.

When Tegan and Sara's song, "Where Does the Good Go," ends, Cristina turns to leave the on-call room, and before she walks out the door, she turns around and says to Meredith:

"You are a gifted surgeon with an extraordinary mind. Don't let what he wants eclipse what you need. He's very dreamy, but he's not the sun. You are."

But no matter how true my mom's saying is, how genius Shonda Rhimes' scripting is, or how dreamy they really are, it seems that it's always the starkest and most hard-hitting advice that helps us understand the importance of doing what's best for ourselves in any relationship.

Fast forward to the end of my sophomore year at Temple, after losing the house and after I'd already committed to ROTC (that story is up next!).

I began making plans to move cross-country to live with my college boyfriend. After graduating from the Air Force Academy, he was stationed at Holloman Air Force Base in Alamogordo, New Mexico. As things continued to be hard for my family it felt like a chance to run away.

I called the ROTC detachment commander and the journalism department head at New Mexico State University to schedule time to speak with each of them during one of my visits.

The plan, as my boyfriend and I discussed, was that I'd transfer schools and ROTC detachments and finish out my schooling in New Mexico. We'd live part way between the base and Las Cruces, where NMSU is located.

This would allow us to live together after having been long distance between Colorado Springs and Philadelphia our entire relationship, even though we were from the same hometown. By the time I'd graduate, we figured we could be talking about getting married and moving to the same Air Force base together.

Everyone I knew tried to talk me out of it but I carried on with my well-designed plan for a future.

I remember the day I walked around the NMSU campus.

I dropped him off at work at the base and took the Volvo to Las Cruces. When I arrived at the campus, I put myself in visualization mode, walking around all day imagining myself walking the walkways and sitting in the classrooms and looking around at the desert scenery.

I met with the ROTC detachment commander and the rest of the staff and discussed the transition from Temple to NMSU and where I'd fit into the detachment. I walked from the detachment to the communications school through the quiet hallways to the administration office.

I sat down in a woman's office, one of the administrators, in a chair across the desk from her. We talked about the school and the journalism degree program and my education opportunities. She answered my questions about credits and scheduling and my expected graduation date. She asked me about myself and Temple and about living in Philly.

And then she looked me dead in the face and said,

"I have to ask. Are you an idiot?"

"*Excuse me?*" I said.

"I'm sorry if that comes across as rude," she said, "but I just can't seem to understand this. Sarah, this is New Mexico, and there's not a whole lot going on here. You could transfer here and take our journalism program and do ROTC, but you live in a major city and you're so far into your degree at one of the best journalism schools in the country."

As if her first question wasn't hard-hitting enough, then she said,

"Are you sure you're going to marry this guy?"

My gut reaction was a plain and simple, "No."

I loved him. But I wasn't sure.

I wasn't sure about *anything* in my life in those years.

I left that woman's office and walked to the car. I drove myself to a Starbucks, got a coffee, and sat outside on the patio and chain-smoked cigarettes until I could muster up the courage to get in the car, and make the drive home to what I knew in my heart was going to be the end of my relationship.

We stayed together for a while after that trip, and I never had the heart to tell him what that woman said that day on the campus. But I felt like it was one of those stark, hard-hitting signs.

In the almost decade that has passed since that moment, I've met too many people who stay in a relationship because it's too difficult to leave and do what's best for themselves.

And for some reason we do that to ourselves.

We stay too long, we stay when it's wrong, and we stay because to leave would hurt too much. We stay because we think we're not enough, or because we don't think we could ever do better, or that we deserve more.

We change jobs, move from city to city, get married, have babies, and ruin families before we decide for ourselves to leave when it's not right.

It's not easy to walk away, especially from someone you love. And it's even harder—at least for me it was—to do so when things are good. There was nothing wrong with our relationship, we loved each other so much that it often got the best of us both.

For me, though, I felt something deeper, something more—something calling me. And for that reason, I couldn't stay. I wanted to, because I knew that together we could've had an amazing life.

But my heart was pulling me in a different direction.

*If I move to New Mexico*, I thought, *I'll be giving up on every dream I've ever had for myself.*

In the middle of the crisis that was my family life, and not having any idea what my future had in store, leaving this relationship felt like I was walking away from the one thing I was certain I cared about.

At the same time, I knew in my heart I couldn't care more about somebody else than I needed to care about myself during that time. And I couldn't run away from my life.

I regretted the decision of leaving that relationship for years. I'd get pangs of loneliness and feelings that maybe I'd made the wrong choice and thrown away a perfect love story. But as time passed and things changed for me, I found solace in the fact that putting my life back together was the very reason I left.

I needed to know—for myself—that I knew how best to take care of myself and grab hold of my future.

Call me headstrong, but I didn't want to need somebody else so badly that I gave up needing to have a life of my own choosing.

My mom always says, "When we know better we do better," but I don't always think that's the case. If we know better, we *should* do better, but too often we think we can't.

For me, I've always tried to believe that it's absolutely possible that there's something even greater on the horizon.

No matter what's happened in life, in every situation, I've always tried to hold onto hope.

Too often we forget that while our lives are short, the *rest* of our lives is a long time. And that he or she is not the sun.

You are.

# Revelation 6:

## *You don't have to take the elevator all the way to the basement, you can get off at any floor.*

For every fork in the road, there are often two paths from which to choose: the one you "should" take and the one you want to take. Take the second. Always take the second.

I did,
The Universe

I walked into the detachment in workout shorts, an Air Force hoodie my boyfriend gave me, and my hair in a ponytail. In the waiting area there was a young guy and his dad, both of them in suits with manila folders in their laps.

All I had with me was my phone and my car keys.

Supposedly you should dress up for these meetings as if it were a job interview, but that's how out of place and desperate I was in this whole join-the-military process.

The one superlative I didn't win in high school but should have was, "Least likely to join the military."

But once Mitchell declared he'd be a Marine and went down the path of enlisting, I strongly considered the possibility for myself, too.

My mom always says, "You don't have to take the elevator all the way to the basement, you can get off at any floor."

The way I saw it, I was headed straight for that basement.

It wasn't the fact that I was paying for college with student loans—that's what most of us do. It was more so the fact that I was having such a hard time visualizing what my future would look like given everything that was happening with my family.

On top of the loans, I had two jobs. I was stressed out all the time, severely depressed about how heavy everything felt, I had a boyfriend that lived across the country, and I genuinely had no idea what I wanted for my future.

What was even possible for me now?

I'd latched onto the idea of becoming a brain surgeon early on in life. That's what happens when you ask a kid what they want to be when they grow up.

I didn't come from money and learned quickly the generalization that doctors, especially surgeons—and especially brain surgeons—make a lot of money.

Genius thinking, I know.

I used to joke to my parents, "One day when I'm a brain surgeon I'll make sure I give you both a good discount to remove the crazy."

So I enrolled at Temple as a biophysics major and hated every single day of class. Math and science were never my strengths and I struggled early on to maintain good grades.

I don't remember the process of changing my major or how I went about choosing, but before going into my sophomore year I took a complete right turn and double majored in political science and journalism.

It was immediately apparent I'd made the right switch. I loved what I was learning and my mind was constantly focused on making a difference in the world.

But this still didn't mean I had any sort of direction, and for the most part, I was a terrible writer and even worse public speaker.

I constantly struggled with thinking, *How will I ever be able to afford the life I want to live? What does that life even look like now?*

Inspired by my baby brother's big decision, I dove in and learned as much as I could about the military. *How badass would it be to be a Marine?* I thought.

The concept taught in all military basic training is that you break everyone down to de-emphasize their individuality, and then you rebuild them collectively to emphasize the value of teamwork.

I craved that so badly for my life.

How could I break everything down until there's nothing left and then just start over and begin anew?

So I tagged along with Mitch one day to the recruiter's office in Allentown. After sitting with a Marine recruiter asking questions about what it would look like for me to join, he said, "Well yeah, sure, you could enlist in the Marine Corps. But you're already in college so you might as well do ROTC and become an officer and make more money."

ROTC?

Officer?

More money?

I had no idea what he was talking about. I'd never heard these terms before, let alone what they could mean for me.

He explained that the Reserve Officer Training Corps is a program in which college students can earn a scholarship to pay for their four-year degree and, in turn, they commit themselves to four years of active duty to the branch of service they did ROTC for.

Because you graduate with a college degree, you commission as an officer as opposed to an enlisted military member.

This is a generalization, but to keep it as simple as possible, officers make up about 10 percent of each military branch's total personnel. They are tasked to serve as leaders of enlisted service members, who generally work in assigned career specialties and, because they make up that remaining 90 percent of military personnel, are the backbone of the force.

I left the recruiter's office that day with a call in to the University of Pennsylvania's Navy and Marine Corps ROTC detachment.

Several weeks later I was in West Philadelphia filling out paperwork, performing a fitness test, and getting ready to sign my name and my life away to the Marine Corps.

The military officer career that aligned best with my new journalism major was Public Affairs Officer. When I showed up at Penn that day, it was explained to me that it can take a long time to be a Public Affairs officer in the Marines, but that in the Air Force you can be a PAO straight out of college when you first enter active duty.

So that's how I found myself at St. Joseph's University, Detachment 750 instead, in my shorts and hoodie, shaking hands with the commander and leaving the building with uniforms in my hands and the title of Cadet Bergstein.

I went home to Miss Kathy that night and put on my uniform for her. She cried as she took pictures of me and gushed about how proud she was that I was staying in school and making this choice for my future.

To this day, when I lace up my boots and see myself in the mirror in my uniform it feels somewhat surreal. *How did I get here?* I find myself wondering from time to time.

But all those years ago, this 20-year-old girl had an opportunity to create a sense of stability and security for her future.

I think back to the incredible chance I was given—

Before I was officially deemed a cadet, I got called into the detachment to talk to one of the cadre members, Major MacEachern.

He had me stand at attention across from his desk while he proceeded to tell me that it was decided by headquarters that they didn't feel it was best for someone like me to be an ROTC cadet.

I'd gotten in trouble for underage drinking several times in high school, and the headquarters personnel felt that, with my record, I wasn't the caliber of person the Air Force was looking for.

I stood there in absolute shock.

*This* was my rock bottom.

Things had been so bad for so long that I felt like joining the military was my only hope for a future. Now, because of a few dumb mistakes I'd made in high school, I wasn't even good enough to join the military.

Major Mac, as everyone referred to him, let me stand there in silence for a few moments before he spoke again. He had me stand at ease so I could look directly at him and told me that when he got word of their decision, he'd made a call.

He called back to headquarters and explained to them that he felt as though I had a really good shot at being a high-performing cadet, and maybe even one day being a great Air Force officer. He strongly suggested to them that they reconsider their decision, based only on his hunch.

And they said yes.

"I stuck my neck out for you and got you this second chance," he said. "If you so much as get a parking ticket in these next four years, you're done."

In that moment, it was official. I was Cadet Bergstein.

I was horrible at marching, clumsy with orders, and just all around out of place in my first few weeks of ROTC.

But within several months of becoming a cadet I'd earned a full scholarship to pay for the remaining three years I'd attend college plus a stipend that helped me pay for living expenses.

You can bet Major Mac made me earn that scholarship.

Not counting my blessings too quickly, I still kept two jobs—the one at the Diner and a bartending job in the city—for the extra money.

I don't think I fully appreciated it at the time because I was just so desperate for things to get better, but I realize now that I was fortunate to be given a second chance, and that second chances don't come often in life.

What's more, it wasn't simply handed to me, but rather, I had to earn my place.

Who knows if that elevator really ever was headed for the basement for me, but looking back now, I'm sure glad I was able to get off before it got anywhere close.

# Revelation 7:

## *Sometimes you're in the right place at the right time and all you can do is pay it forward.*

To touch someone with kindness, is to change someone forever.
Heavy, huh? That's nothing. Because for everyone you touch, you
also reach everyone they will ever know. And everyone they
will ever know. And everyone they will ever know. And so,
for the rest of all time, your kindness will be felt, in waves
that will spread, long after you move on.

Muchas gracias,
The Universe

In my first two and a half years on active duty I was stationed on the island of Guam, where I lived in a condo complex that was right next to a gorgeous Sheraton hotel. It had an infinity pool and this incredible glass-housed chapel, all on a cliff that overlooks the ocean. It was such a beautiful place and made for the best sunset photos.

So when I'd had the occasional really long day at work, I'd drive straight to the Sheraton parking lot, still in uniform with my camera in hand, and would head out to the pool to watch the sun set.

One evening I stood at the balcony overlooking the ocean and a man was standing there beside me. We made small talk about the view and how wonderful the island is. We talked more about the island and travel and a bit about my job in the Air Force.

People who know me well know that I've completely disregarded that whole don't-talk-to-strangers thing that my parents really did teach me when I was a kid.

I talk to anyone and everyone, and will start up a conversation in the most random of places.

I've always considered it one of my biggest strengths and one of the things I love most about myself.

Being open to a conversation with just about anyone is the reason for so many of the most memorable moments of my life.

The sun had just set and my new acquaintance, John, looked over at me and said, "So look, I know it's such a long flight home from here and that it's really expensive to travel from Guam."

He went on to tell me he was an airline pilot with 23 years of flying experience with the airline and eight years of flying with the Marines.

"My wife flies for free and my kids do, too, and every year I get these buddy passes. I want to give one of them to you."

I don't have a clue what I said to him at this point or if I even replied. I very well could have stood there staring at him and not uttered a word.

"You can use this pass however you want. Use it to fly home, bring somebody out here, or take a vacation and go travel somewhere."

Was this guy for real? I was probably still silently staring at this point.

"So here's what I'm going to do," he said. "I'll give you my email address, and you keep that on hand, and whenever you're ready to book your trip, you just reach out to me and let me know and I'll help you do it."

I'm tearing up at this point.

"Oh my gosh. This is so nice."

Finally I'd found my words.

"Why are you doing this for me?" I asked.

He said something that, word for word, I've never forgotten.

"You know, Sarah, sometimes you're in the right place at the right time and all you can do is pay it forward."

My sister Jaclyn and I had grown closer than ever before in the years that we were at Temple and in ROTC together before both becoming Air Force officers.

It was incredible we went to the same college together and that she, also inspired by Mitch, decided to join the Air Force, too.

Leaving home to be stationed on Guam was hard because it meant that I was so far away from my baby sister and best friend.

So I left that hotel, with my camera and a piece of paper with an email address on it in hand, and I called Jaclyn from the parking lot.

"Hey sis. Want to come live with me on Guam for a few months?"

At the time, Jaclyn was living at home waiting to get the call to report for active duty. Back then, ROTC cadets would commission and have about a six-month wait before getting called to report to their first duty station. In Jaclyn's case, she was having to wait a whole year. That's a year of technically being unemployed before owing several years of service, which makes it hard to make any kind of life plans.

That said, it didn't take much convincing when I told her I had a free round-trip ticket to fly her to Guam and that she could live with me for free the next several months. She flew out in October and we both went home for Christmas together that year.

John did exactly what he said he would do. I emailed him and he helped me put her travel together, and then he went one step further.

Turns out, back in the States he lived about an hour away from our hometown in Pennsylvania and when we booked Jaclyn's trip, he met her and my parents at Chris' Diner, then drove her the two hours to New York to help her catch her flight. Because he was flying that day, he was just on his way to work and figured he'd make sure she got on her flight.

He walked her to her gate, made sure everything was squared away, and kept me updated on her travel once she was on her way.

In the months Jaclyn lived with me on the island she got SCUBA certified and we went diving almost every weekend. We hiked the island, jumped off waterfalls, went to island fiestas, and watched the sun rise and set together. She even got to spend time on the base shadowing the security forces squadron, since that was the job she'd be doing once she got on active duty.

It was two of the most incredible months we'd had together and we talk about it all the time to this day.

People thought I was crazy when I told them the story about how Jaclyn got to come live with me. Sadly, they said things like the guy was just hitting on me or that there was some kind of catch or that he wanted something in return.

While unfortunately that does happen in life, those things *never once* crossed my mind while I stood there and received an incredibly selfless gift from a complete stranger.

John the Pilot reinforced something for me that I've always believed: that there are so many good people in the world.

We're taught to keep our guard up, not to talk to or trust strangers, and to protect ourselves, and rightfully so—I suppose—to a point.

I prefer to continue believing that people are inherently good.

People like Cap'n John, as I call him, make that belief possible.

While my parents are thankful I've developed more street smarts today than I may have had during that time when I was young (and we typically think we're invincible), it's always been my first instinct to trust someone as a decent human no matter what.

I hope I never lose that.

# Revelation 8:

## *Why not you?*

Contrary to popular thinking, being worthy isn't something you
earn, it's something you recognize. And once you do, you won't
be able to think, speak, or behave in any other way than as
if what you most wanted was meant to be.

You were born worthy,
The Universe


At one point I thought maybe I wanted to be the Mayor of
Philadelphia. After spending my first year of college getting to
know the North Philly area, I knew there was so much I could
do to help.

*If I had a platform like the mayor*, I thought, *then I could
create so much positive change for the city and the people who
lived there.*

"What makes you think these people want or need your help,
Sarah?" my dad asked one day while driving me back to
Allentown from campus.

So I wouldn't have to drive, my dad picked me up regularly
from the Lansdale train to work at the Diner on the weekends
in my freshman year.

In the 45 minutes it took to get home from the train, I'd ramble
on and on about the plight of the city and my ideas for fixing
it.

"Sarah, one day you'll become jaded like the rest of us," he
said.

It pierced me right in the heart.

And in that moment in the car just down the street from our old house, I swore to myself that I'd never, ever, in my lifetime, allow myself to be hardened by the world.

I refuse to believe that things stay the way they are in the world—and in life—because that's how they've always been and always will be.

I believe that one person *can* make a difference.

I wasn't mad at my dad for what he said. I just thought he wasn't a dreamer anymore. I've realized it happens to a lot of people along the path of life.

We grow up being told how we should live our lives and all the things we need to do to ensure we're safe, secure, and comfortable.

So I think we move through life learning to seek out comfort, and while we're doing that we look at the world around us—as harsh and cruel as it can be—and it affirms that we should continue to play it safe.

But at 19 years old, I told myself, *I'll never be jaded like anybody else.* And with this notion I've continued to dream.

Along the way I've met so many of the, "I've always wanted to, but…" kinds of people.

When you're in the military people often tell you, "I was going to join the military, but…"

And then there are the people *in* the military who say, "I really wanted to do *X* or become *Y* in life…but I've just decided to stay for the full 20 years of service and get my retirement."

I meet more people who've given up on their dreams than I have people who've truly gone for it, but I do my very best to keep on dreaming.

Because here's the thing:

*Why not you?*

Scientists have calculated the odds of you being born. And as much as I'd love for you to think I discovered this research on my own, I didn't. I learned it from a woman who inspires me to no end.

Mel Robbins shares this research in her now famous TED Talk, "How to stop screwing yourself over."

According to Mel, scientists have run the numbers and took into account wars, natural disasters, and everything else, and determined that the odds of you being born, at the moment you were born, to the parents you were born to, with the DNA you have, and determined you have a:

1 in 400,000,000,000,000

Yes, a one-in-four-hundred-TRILLION shot at being here.

As Mel says, "You're not fine, you're fantastic! You have life-changing ideas for a reason, and it's not to torture yourself."

I'd love if after you put this book down you'd take 20 minutes and watch what is one of my favorite TED Talks of all time.

After the talk went viral it eventually led to her publishing her book, *The 5 Second Rule*, which has become a massive movement that helps people change their lives in five seconds at a time.

With my entrepreneurial brain, I have ideas all day long. It's typical for me to have thought of 10 new business ideas or inventions before I've even had dinner each day, and I'm constantly looking at ways to improve myself and the world around me.

But my ideas and your ideas are no good if not acted upon.

About a year ago I was complaining to my boyfriend, Chris, about how I had hundreds of blog ideas written down in various notebooks…but I wasn't actually blogging.

He said, "Tomorrow you're going to compile that list and you're going to send it to me so I can hold you accountable to it. Sarah, I don't want you looking back on your life with hundreds of ideas all stuffed in notebooks."

And that's the same thing I don't want for you.

What is your big dream? What's the one dream you have that's so big that people would literally laugh at you if you told them?

Yep, that's the one I'm talking about.

Don't let that go.

Don't shy away.

Don't see it as being too hard or too far away or too complicated or too big.

Instead, see it as a chance—just as unique as you being here on this planet is—and chase it with everything you have.

Why did I ever want to be the Mayor of Philadelphia? It wasn't for the politics, at all.

What I really wanted was the platform to be able to stand before a city of more than a million people and share with them that their unique gifts matter.

That what they want for themselves, their lives, and for their families is attainable. I wanted to help people overcome their obstacles, turn their lives around, and turn their city around, too.

This was even before my family struggled so severely with the loss of the house. If anything, those events now make my desire to reach others even stronger.

Now don't mistake me—my dad is the most incredible father in the world. He's always been right there beside me through every single thing I've ever done in my life. He's loving, extremely caring, and has taught me so many important things. He's one of my biggest supporters and I will always be a daddy's girl.

But his words that day in the car on the drive home from school were wrong. Especially because he and my mom have always encouraged me to chase my dreams.

So to set the record straight, here's some better advice:

Don't become jaded like the rest of them. Promise me, and more importantly—promise yourself—that you won't be hardened by the world.

You don't want to be looking back on your life with hundreds of ideas all stuffed in notebooks, either.

So ask yourself often, *Why not you?*

After all, you never know. I just might be the Mayor of Philadelphia one day.

*Why not me?*

# Revelation 9:

## *Too much negativity in one day is like a bad hangover.*

A Paradoxical Perspective from your friend, the Universe:
On earth, it seems that most people fret, worry, and lose
sleep over some of the silliest things they've done. But what's
funny is that later on, from here, more often than not, it's the
things they didn't do that they still think about.
Which of course sends them back.

Tallyho, ho, ho,
The Universe

I can't help but sometimes feel like I have been late to the game in life.

I was born late. I was late to apply to college. I was late to change my major. I was late to sign up at ROTC. I was late to figure out my health. I was late in starting my business. I was late in writing this book.

And I am somehow always late to everything.

Or… has everything been exactly and perfectly on time?

Sitting in an AA meeting is some of the best therapy I've ever had. As I've had experience with traditional therapy, too, I've learned the two could never compare.

"I need a meeting!" I used to gasp to my mom whenever I was going through something hard at school or with friends or a boyfriend in my high school years.

While the topic was about alcohol and early on I couldn't necessarily relate to the experiences of a lot of the people in The Rooms, the topics of love, fear, failure, faith, relationships, trust, strength, grace, humility, etc., are all universal, and so I learned to take from the stories what applied to me and what was relatable to exactly where I was in my own life.

I admit that I've always been a self-help junkie. And it started in middle school.

Back when MySpace was a thing, my page was filled with inspirational quotes, mantras, and life lessons. When my time on the computer was limited to what my parents would allow for each of us to share the family computer and dial-up internet, I spent all of that time looking at quote websites, reading inspirational stories, and finding uplifting words to encourage me.

I had quote books, quote calendars, and all kinds of things with quotes written on them, and I was always surrounding myself with these little gems of positivity.

Once I was old enough to drive and had my own car, I'd spend hours at the local Borders or Barnes & Noble bookstores combing through the self-help shelves for anything and everything I could get my hands on. I loved reading inspirational books and stories, and every how-to about making your life better in any way spoke directly to me.

The older I got and the less I went to meetings with my mom, the more obsessed I became with personal development. And that obsession has continued ever since.

It has occurred to me all these years later that the reason I craved these meetings so much, aside from always wanting to be around my mom, was that while I was in the meeting, and long after going to one, I always felt a sense of peace.

I'm no therapist, but I believe that I've longed for and craved that positivity so badly, then and now, because it was what fueled me as a kid.

I felt better after I went to meetings. Years later, I still find myself looking for that *thing*, that something that helps me find that same sense of peace when life gets tough.

It would surprise most people who know me to know that I suffer from, at times, pretty severe depression and anxiety.

To everyone else, I'm always the happy, energetic, positive one.

And that's very true. I'm mostly a genuinely happy person, but I'm a first-class worrier too. Find me something to worry about and I will kick that around in my head until kingdom come.

And then I'll worry about how much I worried about it.

When that worrying spirals out of control, the aftermath leaves me in a deep and achy depression.

In my search for healing, I've talked to therapists. I've tried depression and anxiety medications. I've journaled, read, walked, slept, meditated, bathed, incensed, cooked, and exercised my way through it all, but what I've found to work best in keeping me out of the funk is having a clear, actionable, manageable list of things to do that are directly in alignment with my purpose and what I most want.

Now what the heck does that even mean?

Me feeling "late to the game" in life? That's me being extremely hard on myself and always holding myself to insanely high—and sometimes unrealistic—standards.

So it took me a long time to recognize that there are certain triggers that make me anxious, and thus depressed.

While on active duty, it was that I didn't have enough hours in a day to work on my passion in health coaching and helping others.

I find that I get incredibly anxious when I spend too much time scrolling on social media, if I binge-watch Netflix, or if I eat out or am off my normal eating habits for too many days in a row.

I used to get anxiety all the time from drinking, but we'll get to that later.

I get anxious when I don't exercise and move my body in some way daily.

And lately, I get anxious about the success of my business and my life as an entrepreneur. We'll definitely get to that, too.

All of those things are not necessarily things to stress about, but when I reach that point of "too much" for me, I ultimately end up feeling really badly if I don't change my mindset, actions, or habits somewhat quickly.

Because here's the thing—it's incredibly easy to feel like crap.

There's a lot to worry about in the world and dozens of ways we can compare ourselves to those around us and feel that perhaps we're not enough.

I've always loved the question asked by Dr. Phil, "How's that working for you?"

My mom asked me that question often when I'd come to her in a lousy mood and looking for advice.

"Too much negativity in one day is like a bad hangover," she'd say. "So how's that working for you?"

The comparison game is fierce as technology and social media make it ever easier to be consumed with what everyone else is doing.

The more we're connected to our screens and to each other, the less time we have to be plugged in and connected to ourselves.

And that time to ourselves is more important now than ever before.

The most comforting thing in walking my journey through both the anxiety and depression I sometimes feel, is that it's always temporary, and I am by no means alone.

To a degree, we all get a little anxious and we all get a little down at times. Some of us suffer much more severely than others, but simply knowing I'm not alone in this battle is relief in and of itself.

I sat in silence about everything I had bottled up inside of me for so long and I resisted getting help for years—*years!*

If I could go back and change just one thing in my life it would be putting my ego and pride aside and asking for help whenever I need it, for whatever reason, no matter how silly I felt.

I often need this reminder my mom says from the Bible: "Who of you by worrying can add a single hour to your life? Since you cannot do this very little thing, why do you worry about the rest?"

There's absolutely no reason to suffer any longer than you have to.

Like my mom always says, "Pain is inevitable, misery is optional."

No matter where you are in your journey, if the content of any of these chapters pulls at your heartstrings because you've experienced something similar or have been waiting to seek help, this is me giving you permission to take the first step.

Don't wait like I did.

Because at the end of the day, how's that *really* working for you?

# Revelation 10:

## *Don't take yourself so seriously.*

What if every "no," meant "not yet"? Every setback meant,
"there's something way better"? Every loss meant, "even
more is on the way"? And every disappointment meant,
"pucker up, buttercup"?

Yeah, precisely,
The Universe

I almost titled this book, "No means maybe."

As a journalism major at Temple we were encouraged to get
an internship before graduation. So as I looked around at
where I could intern, my passion was definitely in broadcast
journalism. I always thought it'd be cool to be a news anchor,
so I applied to FOX 29 News in Philadelphia.

I submitted my application and resume and was scheduled for
an interview.

The week of the interview I was having lunch with a girlfriend
on campus between classes, when she asked me about my
interview. I told her it wasn't until the next day.

She was quiet for a minute, until she informed me that I had
my dates mixed up and that the interview was actually to have
taken place that morning…I'd missed it completely.

I've learned over time that life doesn't always prepare you for
certain situations. You just have to take the information you
have at the time and make the best decision based on that.

In this case, I had no idea what the best decision was.

Should I call and reschedule? Should I just forget it altogether and suck it up to a huge loss on my part? Do I ask one of my professors to help me make it right?

I kicked ideas around in my head all day while feeling completely mortified that I'd just blown a huge opportunity. FOX 29 News is not some rinky-dink station, and only a handful of people get their shot at this internship.

By the end of the day I'd come up with my plan.

I was going to show up the next day. Since I'd thought my interview was actually supposed to be on that day, I reasoned that this wasn't a complete lie.

It wasn't the best plan, but it was the best I could think of at the time.

The next morning I got ready, put on my nicest news lady clothes, as I called them, hopped on the subway with my little business folder in hand, and made my way to the station.

I buzzed in at the door when I arrived and after the security guard asked me what I was there for I proudly stated, "Hi, I'm Sarah Bergstein and I'm here for my internship interview!"

The man came back on the intercom and said, "I'm sorry, miss, but I'm told by the coordinator that she doesn't have any interviews scheduled for today. She said that your interview was yesterday."

I panicked. This was it. I'd ruined it.

But maybe there was still a chance.

I'd made my decision. I'd gotten dressed up. I went all the way to the station, and at the very least, I felt I owed myself a little more of a push before throwing in the towel.

"I actually legitimately thought my interview was scheduled for today and I apparently got the dates mixed up. I know that she's probably insanely busy and that she has no obligation to meet with me, but can you ask her if I can have just five minutes of her time to do my interview?"

I was sweating like crazy. Thankfully my news lady clothes were black.

I waited at the door for what felt like an eternity until suddenly the door buzzed and unlatched.

I'd been let inside.

"Have a seat and she'll be with you."

I was in.

*Just be yourself. Just be yourself. Just be yourself.* I kept telling myself while I waited.

And when the coordinator came to meet me, we shook hands and walked to her office.

"You know your interview was supposed to be yesterday and you missed it?" she asked.

Crap. Not a good way to start.

"Yes. I know. First mistake I've ever made in 22 years of my life," I joked. "Man, I had a really good track record going for a while there, too!"

It was a huge risk to crack a joke when my dream internship was at stake.

But she let out a really good laugh, and we moved on with the interview.

I walked out of the station that day as a FOX 29 News summer intern, and I was sweaty and beaming and proud.

To this day I still can't believe I pulled that off. The summer I spent there as an intern made for so many experiences and memories that I will never forget.

I'd completely forgotten about the whole story behind how I scored that internship until my mom reminded me one day as we laughed about it on the phone.

That moment had taught me not to take myself so seriously.

While recounting her memory of the story to me my mom said, "You know, Sarah, one of the things I admire about you is that, to you, no means maybe."

The way she explains it, it's like a door is closing and I stick my foot right in front of it just before the door is about to shut.

She was right. I've always lived my life that way. To me, it's only a *no* when you don't ask, don't ask again, or when you give up.

When you really want something in life, like I wanted that fancy internship, when you think somebody might say "no," instead think maybe they'll say "yes."

When there's a lot on the line, put it in your mind that "no" can mean "maybe," and believe and carry yourself like it does.

Maybe a "no" can be a "maybe."

Or maybe a "no" can just be a "not right now."

Or maybe a "no" can be a "yes."

But you'll never know if you don't try to find out.

You'll certainly be told "no" plenty of times in your life. Lord knows I have—it happens all the time.

But I always approach a situation like maybe I won't.

Who knows, perhaps the one "no" you thought you'd get is actually the one "yes" you've been looking for.

# Revelation 11:

## *This is your life.*
## *Write your own script.*

Of course it's true, everyone's born with a gift. One that will
allow them to fill a special place in the Universe that absolutely
no one else can fill. A blessing that makes all other blessings
pale in comparison. A gift of incalculable value to the entire
world when it's uncovered, explored, and embraced.
Yours? Being you.

Tallyho,
The Universe

I was mesmerized by her. She had it all—the "hutzpah" as my
Jewish grandparents would've called it, or the "moxie," as I
like to say.

Candice Adams Ismirle was an energetic, outgoing, smart, and
talented public affairs officer. Within minutes of meeting her,
she became my gold standard of what it meant to be a
successful PAO.

She was one of my instructors at my technical school at Fort
Meade in Maryland in early 2012. The Defense Information
School is where each branch of the military sends its public
affairs personnel to learn their craft.

I was floored by Captain Adams, as she was referred to then,
even before she told us her story. I'd been on active duty for
less than 30 days when she walked into our classroom with so
much energy and charisma. I thought immediately, *This girl is
clearly one of the best in the field.*

She commanded the room with her presence and it was evident she was a well-respected leader and officer. Her fellow instructors couldn't say enough nice things about her, and by the way they all joked around and laughed with one another, it was clear she was well liked by everybody.

After teaching a class on media relations, she sent us on a break and had the projector screen down when we returned.

She proceeded to show us a story called "Pink Kisses: Cancer My Way." The 22-minute video was photographed, filmed, and produced by an Airman, Staff Sergeant Russ Scalf, who documented an 18-month battle with breast cancer—Candice's battle.

While "Triple Negative"—the type of breast cancer Candice was diagnosed with—forms lumps like other forms of breast cancer, it is a very different disease. It's a relatively newly discovered variant, and is particularly deadly because it grows aggressively and there aren't yet many chemotherapy options that are proven effective. As such, the survival rate, especially following a relapse, is very low.

If you met her in passing and hadn't seen this project or heard her story, you'd have never known that, while she'd won, Candice had fought for her life.

It's because she and her husband, Ryan, chose to *celebrate* life, rather than simply *survive* it. Those are her words.

A fighter pilot, known as a leader and a person who can connect with anyone, as she describes him, Candice met Ryan in 2008 at an Air Force training course in Alabama and they were engaged in 2010.

It was five months later that she found the lump.

In May 2011, after chemo and a double mastectomy, Candice was cancer-free and she and Ryan began planning their wedding and bought a house in Washington D.C., as both of them were now stationed at the Pentagon. They married in 2012.

When the cancer came back in 2013 it had spread to Candice's brain, abdomen, lungs, and liver and she underwent brain surgery and more chemo, followed by regular and smaller maintenance doses of chemo each month.

In the wake of these new challenges and after all they'd been through, she and Ryan pressed forward with their dreams of becoming a mom and dad.

They'd experienced miscarriages in the time of her remission, but at the advice of a doctor years prior they'd frozen embryos, as they were and had always been hopeful about the future.

Because Candice's cancer had returned, she was no longer able to carry a baby. So she and Ryan call it a miracle that her cousin, Erin, vowed to be what's called a gestational carrier.

On November 4, 2014, twin boys, Rafe Michael and Ryder Craig were born, and Candice's dream of becoming a mom became her and Ryan's reality.

Today, many of us have been touched by cancer in some way. And in telling you Candice and Ryan's story, this is why it matters so much to me:

Sitting in that classroom back in 2012, Candice offered for all the young female officers to attend a breakout session, where she'd provide mentoring and advice for those of us who had questions about our career paths as public affairs officers.

It was absolutely like her to volunteer her free time like that.

As the girls asked about how best to position themselves, the correct steps to take to follow the perfect career progression, and how to check all the necessary boxes to ensure being considered for the most high-profile and desired positions, Candice looked over the room and said something I've not only never forgotten, but has changed and shaped the way I view my *entire* life, not just my career in the Air Force.

"Here's the thing, ladies," she said. "No matter what, you have to write your own script and chart your own path. No one can tell you what the perfect career path is going to be and you can't be married to it going just that one way, because life doesn't always work like that.

"What you need to do is follow your heart and your dreams and don't let anybody tell you the right or wrong way to navigate your career. You want to be able to make it your own."

Candice's advice, like her presence and joy for life, has stayed with me as my checks and balances for making certain that I'm living a life of my choosing.

She fought like a warrior with grace, dignity, and strength from the very beginning. She gave hope to those fighting similar battles and inspired everyone who was blessed to know her.

Rafe and Ryder were 15 months old when Candice was called home, but her memory is strong in everyone's hearts.

She remains a light in so many people's lives—especially mine.

Candice lit up every room she ever walked into and she didn't just know people or become liked by those she met—she touched every person in a way that is personal to them, and unforgettable to us all.

If you've ever thought one person can't make a difference in the world, you just hadn't had the chance to meet Candice.

Today, Ryan, Rafe, and Ryder live in North Carolina, writing their script with the memory of his wife and their mommy at the forefront.

There are no absolute rules about how you should live your life, but as I've learned from Candice's strength, it's always better to choose to fully live life.

We're each here for a relatively short amount of time and our days are not promised to us.

This is your life.

My wish for you—as Candice encouraged me—is that you choose to celebrate life, rather than simply survive it; that first, now, and always, you chart your own path and write your own script.

# Revelation 12:

## *You're only as sick as your secrets.*

No more "supposed tos," ok? You're not supposed to work harder,
look better, sleep less, sell more, run faster, talk slower, be happier,
stay longer, leave earlier, cook, clean, negotiate, settle, start,
stop, move, try, win, shake, rattle, or roll.
Other people made that all up.

I love you the way you are,
The Universe

It has taken me almost 30 years to find some semblance of balance.

Until recently, I've spent my life struggling with poor body image, self-confidence issues, and lots of negative self-talk about how I looked and felt, and what my body was capable of versus what it allowed me to do.

I had an eating disorder long before I even knew what that really was. If I had to guess, I think it turned into an issue in middle school when I made the middle school cheerleading team. From there, I traveled down a sad and uncomfortable road for many years.

I'm not recovered by any means. Like my mom says, she's a "recovering alcoholic." Even after more than two decades, she's not recovered.

Recovery is a process—one that takes a lot of work to get to a place where you can live happily inside the body you were given.

To a degree, I think we all suffer from body image disorder. We have an idea in our minds of what the ideal body looks like to us, and any little part that doesn't match that idealized perfection causes a bit of discomfort, whether we ever voice it to anyone or it festers inside of us.

I'd argue that everyone has, at one point, stared at our nude bodies and thought about at least one thing we think could be better.

And there's absolutely nothing wrong with wanting to improve unless, as in my case, your whole life begins to revolve around it.

If I had one piece of advice for everyone, it would be to appreciate the body you have and take every opportunity possible to take the best care of it that you can.

I don't have many regrets, but the things that give me a twinge of pain are not starting sooner to learn how best to treat my body, and not asking for help when I desperately needed it.

Today, I encourage everyone to research reputable sources to find out how to eat right, practice moving your body often, participate in activities that help minimize the stress of life and growing up, and always, practice forms of self-care like sleeping, hydrating, avoiding overexposure to the sun, and putting good, clean things in your body.

Looking back, if I'd known education was the answer to my suffering, I like to think I would have suffered a whole heck of a lot less along the way.

As my mom always says, "You're only as sick as your secrets," and as was in my case—the longer you keep them, the sicker you become.

I refused to talk to anyone about my disordered eating habits, just like I did with my anxiety and depression. And so much of those horrible feelings were a direct result of this disorder. Really, one perpetuated the other. So if someone brought it up to me, as my family and friends did over the years, I defended myself like my life depended on it.

When I felt desperate to get help, I told myself I could fix it on my own.

The longer it went on, the more I began to believe I was never going to be happy with my body. I was always going to have to starve myself to look the way I wanted. I'd have to exercise all the time, feel uncomfortable about my body in front of girlfriends and in intimate situations, and believe there was no room for self-love inside of someone who was filled with so much self-loathing.

It's not that I didn't like who I was, but rather, that I mistakenly believed that my outward appearance would make it known that I was a girl who had my life together.

That if I had the right body and could wear all the best clothes and attract all the most handsome guys and coolest friends, that I would always have the most fun, land the right opportunities and the best jobs, and have the upper hand in life.

Middle school, high school, and college came and went and there wasn't one time where I ever felt comfortable in my skin. Looking back at the photos now, as sick as it is, I can tell you exactly how much I weighed in each photo and exactly what methods I was using to control my eating disorder at that time.

Those are years—more than a decade—of my life that I can't get back. Years that I hid behind my disordered body image and habits.

It controlled everything I did, from what I ate, to where I went, to how I made friends, to how I shopped, to the experiences I'd have, to how I viewed myself.

Looking back, I can see now that I used my eating disorder as a form of inflicting pain on myself to deal with everything else. Some people drink their problems away, I tried to starve mine out. Some people cut themselves, I tried living on a diet of coffee and cigarettes.

And every time I'd starve myself or binge eat it was to relieve some form of pain that I was experiencing.

The problems—and even the pain itself—never went away, but the control made me feel alive.

So when I got to Guam for my first assignment, I continued living that way. I ate as little as I could, did as much cardio as possible, and smoked cigarettes and drank like crazy.

It wasn't until December 2012 that I'd really had enough. Maybe it was the same feeling my mom had when she decided to quit drinking.

I told myself that I was literally sick and tired of feeling sick and tired, and that it was time for things to change.

I happened to have seen a photo on Instagram of a girl who, in the left frame of the photo was an average-looking girl, and in the right photo, she was insanely fit. I told myself I wanted that. Whatever *that* was.

So I decided to compete in a figure competition, which I learned was the reason that average girl looked so fit.

It wasn't until that time that I began to open up about the way I'd treated myself for so many years.

And while it was scary to admit those things—just as it is now—I told myself then, that if my story could help one person not suffer the way I did, then it was worth putting myself out there for all the embarrassment I may feel.

I can't get caught up thinking about how much time I wasted—it's maddening for me to even go down that path anymore.

But it's exactly the reason why I became so passionate about helping others make peace with themselves, and to find what works best for them to take care of themselves and love their bodies.

It's not an easy thing, as I've come to learn, and even after I dove into the competition, got my master's degree in exercise science, and became a personal trainer, nutrition specialist, and life coach, I still wasn't "recovered."

Actually, the competition perpetuated a whole new level of disordered body image because everything about me had to be perfect for the stage.

My entire life became about my abs, what I was eating, what time I was going to go to the gym, and what workout I'd be doing.

I told myself that's just what athletes do.

It was an incredibly rewarding experience and a true test of my willpower, strength, grit, and ability to accomplish a goal, but the place it put me in mentally was just as unhealthy as the opposite end of the spectrum I'd been at for so long.

So even after competing, it took me a few more years to find what *normal* looks like for me.

Once I became a coach, I felt the pressure to look incredible all the time so that I truly looked the part. I actually felt like I needed to diet before I could take professional photos so that my pictures would resemble someone who is insanely fit—believing that my clients would hire me based on my body alone.

While I do think that looking the part is an important part of any job, it was literally limiting my ability to help others.

So I continued with challenges, diet plans, workout programs, and chasing the next big thing that would help me get the body I felt I needed to be the trainer I thought my clients wanted.

It wasn't until I created a program, intended for my clients, that I finally found myself falling into a place of balance on my own terms.

At that point, I was working in Tampa, Florida and created this program as a downloadable self-paced program.

When I launched it, I did the program, too. I also took advantage of living in Florida in the winter months and got back into running outside—something I'd always loved when I first began exercising in middle school.

From my own program I saw incredible results. I lost weight, inches, body fat, and looked and felt the best I ever had in my whole life. When I looked in the mirror, I was truly happy with what I saw. And for the first time ever, I felt comfortable in my skin.

I was not the fittest, leanest, strongest, or skinniest I'd ever been, but I was truly happy. I'd found a satisfied balance between doing workouts I enjoy and eating foods that I love but restricted myself from for years.

For the first time I'm not following a diet or a workout plan, and I'm not on a schedule. I'm not weighing myself, measuring myself, or keeping track of my body fat. I like the way my clothes fit, and I'm comfortable when I'm not wearing them.

It has taken me my whole life to get to this point, and now it feels so good that I can't believe I was ever doing it any other way.

I can't believe I struggled so much, suffered so much, and put my mind and body through so much abuse...and for what?

I completely overlooked—all those years—that there was a possibility that I actually could feel incredible and be happy with my body.

Before I began competing, it wasn't even a thought that crossed my mind that there was a better, healthier, less self-sabotaging way.

The only people I opened up to back then about my disordered eating habits and poor self-image were people who suffered the same issues I did. And while it felt good not to be alone in that struggle, we weren't going to be the answer to helping each other get better.

That was a path I had to walk on my own, being honest about the big secret of my life.

So am I "healed?"

Oh gosh, no.

But through all of my education, training, and experience, I've learned so much about what it means to be healthy...for me.

And while all that information out there can tell you the right things to do, none of it matters unless it's built on the foundation of what you think about yourself.

What you think about yourself begins and ends with you, as you might recall the phrase from my mom.

So for me it was an eating disorder, but for you it could be any number of things.

What's your secret?

Don't feel bad about it, because we all have them.

I've yet to meet a person in 30 years who doesn't.

All you have to do to get better is ask for help. And I get it. It's simple. It's just not easy.

Today, though, I hope you can find solace in the fact that you're not alone, you're not a bad person, and it doesn't have to get worse. You can instead help yourself and allow others to help you in getting better.

And when you do get help, realize that there will be people out there that could benefit from your help, too.

You're only as sick as your secrets—but remember—you don't have to stay sick...and it doesn't need to be a secret.

# Revelation 13:

## *Miracles happen every single day.*

You are not meant to bear that which you find unpleasant.
You are meant to change it. That's why you feel it. Your every
twitch of pain and malaise invites you to wake up, pushing
you to seek grander truths that will reveal a bigger
reality and a more magnificent you, ever closer to an
awareness of your true place within reality
creation – as a Creator.

Boom,
The Universe

As she was finishing up dinner she walked into the restroom
and found a woman crying. Not just quietly having a peaceful
cry, but sobbing like she'd never been hurt so badly before in
her life.

Her first instinct was to ball up a bunch of toilet paper and tend
to her.

Was she ok?

Was she hurt?

Did she need to call someone?

Did something happen and she needed help?

When my mom asked and all those questions elicited "no," she
did the thing she knows how to do best; she stood there in
front of a perfect stranger crying in a restaurant bathroom and
asked her, "Do you need a hug?"

The woman fell right into my mom's arms, wrapping her arms around her and sobbing into her, quietly thanking God under her breath over and over again.

As the woman settled, my mom gave her more tissues, rubbed her arms, confirmed that she'd be ok, and then quietly left the bathroom to leave the woman in peace.

I cried when she told me this story. It had been more than a week since it happened and my mom just happened to have recalled it while we were sitting at the kitchen table having dinner together.

I cried because I felt sad for this woman, but also because I felt an immense wave of pride for what an incredibly loving and giving person my mom is.

Stories like these make life seem a little less harsh to me. My mom has always been the one person in my life that has made me feel like it's not a big, scary, cruel world, after all.

A few months later, I got lucky on the morning I had to fly to Santa Monica, California for work.

They were taking volunteers to get bumped to a flight that departed an hour later but had no layover and would actually get me to Los Angeles International Airport sooner than my original flight. The voucher was for $500 and I knew the following year had a lot of travel in store for me…so I took it.

The flight was full so I was lucky to get an aisle seat in the back of the plane. I used to only sit in the window seat so I could watch out the window, but now I always like to get up more than is probably normal to go to the bathroom and be on my feet, especially during cross-country flights.

Flying 26 hours to and from Guam a dozen times will do that to you. It has made me extremely antsy on planes.

I got settled in my seat and made small talk with the man in the window seat. When the woman who was assigned to sit between us got to the back of the plane, she struck me as being very odd.

We were flying out of Tampa, Florida and she was wearing a heavy puffy winter coat and had with her only a purse. When she sat down between us she didn't say a word. Didn't take out her phone. Didn't fumble around trying to get settled.

She just sat with her hands in her lap and seemed extremely nervous.

I'd love to say something cool like that my military background gives me a sense about people when something is off. But in today's world, I don't think I'm alone in believing that you could be a victim of terrorism, especially when you see somebody acting irregularly on a plane.

Now I know you probably weren't expecting me to say *that*, but this is exactly what I was thinking. Immediately I had a funny feeling about this woman's behavior.

When the plane took off I set my seatback screen to the map of the U.S. so I could see where we were en route.

She tapped me and pointed to her screen as if to ask me to put that on her screen, too. While I wondered if she spoke English, she proceeded to sit with her hands in her lap staring at the screen.

At one point I caught out of the corner of my eye that her hands were folded and she was mouthing prayers.

You'd think maybe I would've thought she was scared of flying and asked her if she was ok, but I was genuinely freaked out by this lady and was running scenarios in my head of how best to tackle her if she tried to set off a bomb.

I thought about saying something to the flight attendants, thinking of the instructions, "If you see something, say something." Right?

I was having major stress over this lady.

So to give myself a moment to breathe, I got up to go to the bathroom. As I waited in line at the back of the plane, she walked up behind me and stood there, too.

Why she chose me or what prompted her to say it, I'll never know, but she leaned into me—this perfect stranger waiting for the bathroom on a plane—and she said, "My son died and that is why I am going to LA."

I immediately felt like a horrible person.

In shock, I said, "I'm so sorry," and hurriedly swapped places with the person in the bathroom and gasped as I locked the door.

My mind was racing and I had no idea what to say. I stayed in the bathroom longer than I needed to, just to piece my thoughts together.

Of course, it made sense now—the nervous movements, the sitting and staring at the back of the seat, the praying and watching the flight pattern. Nothing with her but her coat and purse.

This woman was going through the worst nightmare of her life—all alone—at the back of a plane, sitting between two strangers for five hours at 35,000 feet in the air.

I stood at my seat and waited for her to return to hers.

When she got back to our row my mind flashed to my mom and the woman in the bathroom.

"Would you like a hug?" I offered.

And she fell into my chest and sobbed right there in the aisle of the plane.

The people around us must've thought it was so strange, but I could feel her heartache like it had transferred into my body, too. And we just stood there so she could cry and not have to feel alone.

When we sat back down I got the woman some water, lots of tissues, and spent some time rubbing her arm.

I never thought compassion came to me so naturally like that, but in that moment I felt like I was *exactly* the person we all want to be...that I realized we all have the capacity to be. I made a mental note that I wanted to live my life more fully in this way.

She took out her phone and showed me photos of her son and told me all about her family and the things they'd recently been through.

Her daughter had just gotten married and she couldn't have been happier.

Her son—not even sure yet of how he passed away—owned and operated two 7-Elevens in Florida, and was her first and only son and her pride and joy.

Sadly, her husband had just recently passed away. He was in India visiting family and he suffered a heart attack on the way home.

Just before that, her mother- and father-in-law, who lived with them in the same house for decades, both had recently passed away, too.

I thought to myself, *How does one person deal with so much loss?*

We sat together in silence for the last bit of the flight. My hope was that I'd lifted the weight of some of her sadness for just a little while before things were about to get harder for her.

Upon landing, she was due to go to the morgue to identify her precious son.

I waited for her at the gate when I got off the plane so I could ask her if she needed help finding a ride or if she wanted me to go with her wherever she needed to be.

She assured me that she'd be ok, and then she wrapped her arms around me and whispered in my ear, "I love you," and without a moment of hesitation I told her that I loved her, too.

After we'd parted ways, I happened to be standing nearby when she joined up with her sister in the terminal. You couldn't miss their sadness and the sounds of their sorrow. The woman saw me and walked her sister over, who threw her arms around me for a hug. She wasn't speaking English, but I could feel the gratitude in her words.

Just before I walked out of baggage claim I noticed the two sisters meet up with the rest of their family. It was a group of about a dozen people and they were all sobbing. I thought to myself that I wish I could have met her son. From their sadness I could tell he was an incredible young man, and well loved by so many people.

My mom showed me how to have compassion through her actions.

I thought about John the Pilot, "...all you can do is pay it forward."

I may never see this woman again, but I certainly won't ever forget her, her sister, her family, or her son.

She reminded me that within our physical bodies, we're all carrying around some degree of struggle and sorrow—and that it's often difficult to tell what someone is going through by looking at their exterior.

She reminded me not to judge people so harshly.

She reminded me that, while the world can sometimes be a cruel and scary place, miracles happen every single day by ordinary people, and that at any time, life can call on you to be somebody's miracle.

She was certainly mine.

# Revelation 14:

## *What you think about,*
## *you bring about.*

Relax. Breathe in deep. Hold it. Let it out. Loosen your
shoulders. Smile. Close your eyes. You'll be surprised at
how many voices you'll hear, whispering sweet
encouragement into your ear.

Kissey, kissey, you can do it,
The Universe


I met a monk at the gym.

He was a tall, lean, white-haired and bearded man with the softest eyes, dressed in gym clothes and sneakers with ankle-high socks, and a towel around his neck.

My personal trainer, Steve, introduced me to him as he was leaving from his training session and I was beginning mine.

Dadaji came into my life in a period where everything was changing.

I was working on my master's degree, studying to become a personal trainer and nutrition specialist, was training for a bodybuilding competition, and was finding my way in the world as an Air Force officer with massive dreams and a calling inside me for something more.

As we shook hands and briefly chatted, he told me he taught people how to meditate.

He was different in every way from the idea I'd had in my mind of what a monk should be—what he'd look like, how he'd dress, how he'd talk, all in addition to the fact that I was talking with him in a gym and not watching him meditate in a monastery.

So when he invited me to learn how to meditate, I said, "Absolutely, yes."

He drew a map to his meditation center located on a small road in a fairly central part of the island.

On Guam, it was normal to be given directions like, "Go down the street until you see the statue of the water buffalo, then make a left at the fruit stand, and keep going until you see the really tall coconut palm surrounded by a bunch of banana trees."

The night of my first meditation class I put on comfortable clothes, grabbed a notebook and pen, and hopped in my car with the monk's drawing to his house set on my passenger seat.

He told me to drive up on the lawn and park my car in the grass in front of the house, and when I went inside, the main living space was empty aside from a couch, a large area rug, and a couple of pillows. The windows were open and the sound of the breeze swept through the room. It was pleasantly warm, had a fragrance like scented oils, and felt very inviting.

There were several people that came to that class but I can't even remember their faces when I try.

I felt called there for a reason and was mesmerized by Dadaji the monk, who was no longer in gym clothes and sneakers, but was dressed in a long, saffron orange robe and sandals, just like my stereotypical idea of how a monk should look.

Dadaji has a kind and gentle manner and a laugh that makes you laugh along. I couldn't believe he offered these meditation classes for free. He'd explained that for thousands of years, meditation was always given freely, just like the air we breathe. He said instead of spending from your wallet, that you have to give your time.

He had been a successful certified public accountant (CPA) until he'd decided that rather than settling into a life with a wife and family, instead, he wanted to teach others. At 34 years old he left everything behind to pursue monastic life.

After his year of seminary training in India, he was sent to Guam. That was back in 1986, and he's spent his years since living on Guam and traveling to Australia, Mainland China, Taiwan, Malaysia, and Bali, hosting intensive workshops and teaching people how to meditate and find peace in their lives.

Daily life on Guam is expensive, so he'd started a small CPA practice. He's both a monk in his saffron orange robe teaching people how to meditate, and also helps Guam families with their taxes.

He described his career combination to me as "perhaps peculiar," and I agree that, certainly, he's not your average monk.

But that made it all the more fascinating to learn from him.

I wrote feverishly as he spoke. Every class opened my eyes more and more to the history, meaning, principles, benefits, and purpose of meditation.

Everything I learned revealed that meditation wasn't about trying to make your mind go blank, like I'd always thought. Rather, the practice I learned from Dadaji was focused on using the mind in a natural way, through both concentration and contemplation.

It's based on the concept that, "As you think, so you become," and that in time, through regular practice, anyone can bring their mind to a state of perfect calm.

At the end of each class we sat in meditation. He strummed lightly on an acoustic guitar while softly singing the mantra, "Ba'ba' Na'm Kevalam." It's literally translated from Sanskrit to mean, "only the name of the beloved," but has also come to mean that love is everywhere and is the essence of everything.

Dadaji had his own, more detailed and rich way to explain the meaning of this mantra. His intention was to make sure that every individual could make the meditation process their own.

The meaning of "Ba'ba'," in its fullest expression, he explained as the state of pure being, an Infinity of Love, Joy, Peace, and unbounded Transcendence. Everyone, he said, with regular practice, will find their own perfection.

"Na'm," he said, is the origin of the word, "name," but means more than just a label. Na'm carries the idea of finding our own experience within and gaining genuine knowledge of our own inner being.

"Kevalam," he said, means the idea of "oneness," a possibility that is different than the ordinary experience of ourselves and the busy world around us.

Dadaji often said to the class, "This is waiting within you, find your own self. Your own inner wisdom is unlimited. *You* are the Infinite."

Just a few sessions in, we gathered at the end of class and sat for meditation. Dadaji strummed on his guitar and softly chanted this mantra, and as I relaxed, in place of hearing him say the words, "Ba'ba' Na'm Kevalam," I was now thinking and repeating the phrase in my head, *In all things there is love.*

He'd said that over time, the mantra would begin to take on its own meaning to each of us. And right there, sitting on my meditation pillow, I discovered for myself my very own revelation.

The experience of learning how to meditate disrupted me. It shook my world and opened up all these other doors to information, thoughts, feelings, and a way of living I never knew existed.

I've heard, "When the student is ready, the teacher will appear." In this case, my peculiar monk appeared in a gym and then taught me how to meditate.

I learned that if you can make space in your mind by clearing your thoughts and quieting all the chatter, it's incredible the amount of peace we can find directly within ourselves.

I love the saying, "What you think about you bring about," because it's true.

For so long I'd been looking outward—for outward experiences, advice from others, and ways to fix myself.

Now I understand—through meditation—how important it is to sit, to be still, to listen, and to trust from within.

There's nothing to fix, just healing to be done.

In my journey through learning how to meditate, I learned a breathing exercise that I'd like to pass along to you.

You can do this exercise any time of day for any reason, and you can repeat it as many times as you'd like throughout the day.

Are you ready to begin?

Follow along with your breath as you read.

First, take a few steady breaths. Don't change your breathing. Just notice the steady rise and fall of your chest and the sound of your breath in and out.

Go ahead and take those breaths.

Now we're going to begin the exercise:

After a good exhale, take a nice, steady, deep breath in to the count of four,

1...2...3...4...

Hold that breath for two seconds,

1...2...

Now go ahead and exhale slowly for six seconds,

1...2...3...4...5...6...

Hold that exhale for two seconds,

1...2...

Now go ahead and repeat that three more times through.

Four seconds in.

Hold for two.

Six seconds out.

Hold for two.

Notice yourself relax while doing this exercise and pay attention to how you feel after.

As you continue to practice this, you can increase your inhales and exhales by two seconds each.

Six seconds in.

Hold for two.

Eight seconds out.

Hold for two.

Keep increasing over time as long as your breath will allow.

I do this exercise in the shower, in the car, while I'm working, as I cook, running errands, whenever I feel stressed, or even before falling asleep at night.

And while doing this practice, I think the phrase, *Ba'ba' Na'm Kevalam.*

Love is everywhere and is the essence of everything.

Or as I like to say, *In all things there is love.*

# Revelation 15:

## *My life is so good I feel like I'm cheating.*

The difference you make in someone else's life, will always be smaller than the difference it will make in your own.

Dang, you gotta love your power,
The Universe

I got my entrepreneurial chops while working at the Diner when I was just 15 years old.

I filled out an application at Chris' Family Restaurant at the recommendation of a really close friend, who said he was making quite a bit of money working the weekend breakfast shifts.

"Chris'," as it's referred to around town, is a really well-known diner in Allentown and has been for many years. It's owned by a Greek man (you guessed it, Chris) and his three sons—all of whom are a staple of the Chris' experience.

Once I got the job, I started by working weeknight dinner shifts in order to earn my Saturday and Sunday breakfast shifts. I shadowed a woman who gave nothing but tough love. She had me greet her customers, take their orders, prepare and deliver to the table their soups and salads, then deliver their meals, recommend dessert, then provide them a check.

She stood over my shoulder with her hands on her hips critiquing every move and ensured the customers knew I was in training.

My cheeks would burn red hot when I'd mess up or say something embarrassing, like the time I asked a truck driver how he wanted his pork chops cooked. She was quick to pounce and let me know loudly in front of him that all pork was cooked well done.

I was 15. What did I know?

But within a few weeks I'd earned my breakfast shifts and my life became a routine of school, cheerleading practice, a Friday night football or basketball game, and Saturdays and Sundays from 8 a.m. to 2 p.m. at the Diner working alongside my friend.

Some of the people I worked with were a little rough around the edges and some of them wouldn't even give me the time of day. There were a few women in the beginning who were tough and unkind and acted like I wasn't even there. Eventually those women would come around, and for the most part, I was close with my coworkers.

I spent a total of nine years as a waitress at Chris'. As I've mentioned, I worked all through high school and during summer breaks all through college. When I graduated, commissioned, and waited six months before getting on active duty and moving to Guam, I worked almost every day of the week to keep me busy, and because I loved it.

In the time I spent working at Chris' I'd developed hundreds of relationships.

The owners were endlessly supportive of my education and career path and always ensured there was a shift for me to take on any time I was home and wanted to work.

All the women I worked with were like a second mom or close friend.

And my customers, well, I could write an entirely separate book on them and all the memories and lessons from the best waitressing job in the world.

I got to know every single one of the regular customers who came into the Diner over the years. I got to be part of people's lives outside of their breakfast order, learning about their families, cheering with them through birthdays and births and crying with them through the hard times and loss.

Chris' Family Restaurant was my second family.

And I had regular customers of my own. People who I'd waited on once and came back again for breakfast and to sit in my section. I was asked all the time about school and cheerleading and college and joining the Air Force and how things were going with my family, siblings, boyfriends, and friends. My customers brought me gifts, left me huge tips, and there was no shortage of the best hugs on earth.

I've always been good at memorizing lists and details. Several months into working there I had the entire menu memorized. I knew what was on it, the prices of every item, and could recite it to customers when asked.

So I got really good at finding ways to increase my tips for every shift. It became like a game for me to try and make more money and reach a new record of tips every weekend.

I noticed early on when I'd memorize my customers' orders, my tips would increase.

And the more people were impressed by it, the more I realized I needed to play that up.

I was an entrepreneur and I didn't even know it.

So—and I'm shaking my head and laughing at myself as I write this—I started making bets with some of my customers for fun.

I'd ask them if they wanted to play a game and bet on their breakfast. People loved the challenge.

I'd tell them if I memorized their entire order and got everything right, including drinks, sides, and dessert, that they'd have to add $5 to their tip for me getting it right. If I messed up even just one detail, they could walk away and leave no tip at all.

If I ever did miss a detail, though, they often left a tip, and the extra $5 anyway.

I make light of it now, but mostly I can't believe I was bold enough to ever play those games. At the time I just wanted to have fun at work, give my customers a good experience, and I needed every penny I could make since my parents made us have a job to pay for the things we wanted.

So I hustled as best I knew how by finding every way possible to make my customers happy and keep the tip pocket of my apron full.

There are so many faces that run through my head when I think about my years working at the Diner and all the memories that were made there.

I was privileged to come into that job as a kid who needed money to pay for a car and clothes and also had a plan to graduate high school and go to college and have my whole life ahead of me.

For so many people I worked alongside, and even for some of the people I waited on, that maybe wasn't the case for them.

I worked with people who had a lot of life issues, single moms busting their butts to raise their kids well, and people who worked at the Diner as a second job for additional money. I waited on people who had health issues or were struggling at work or had concerns about their family.

My mom has this saying that I absolutely love, "My life is so good I feel like I'm cheating."

I've often felt that way, too.

My family wasn't rich, we didn't live in a big house, we didn't have fancy cars or things or go on elaborate vacations. And I had to work for everything I wanted.

Even still, the people I was surrounded by at the Diner taught me grace and humility.

I always felt that the education I got about life and about people was better than anything I was learning in high school. I remember so much more about my interactions with people at the Diner than I remember what I learned in any class I sat through.

I learned that you should never judge a person by their appearance. There were several instances where I'd wait on a pretty rough-looking truck driver or a group of kids or an older person, and would think that they'd likely leave me a crappy tip. I was proved wrong more times than I'm proud to admit.

I learned that when you ask someone how they are, you should really listen and give space for them to tell you. More often than not, customers I'd wait on for the first time—complete strangers—would open up to me about what was going on in their lives. While there wasn't a whole lot I could do but listen, it always seemed like that was enough.

I learned that people are genuinely interested and supportive if you let them in. My repeat customers would remember things I told them, like if I had a big test that week or was going to visit a college or was having a bad day, and they'd follow up and ask me how things were going, often remembering details I'd forgotten I'd told them.

I learned that a simple gesture could change a person's day. I loved writing little notes on the back of my customers' checks or stopping by a table of someone I knew to ask them how they were doing.

And I learned that while I could memorize orders to help me make more money, I made it a point to memorize my repeat customers' orders because I cared about them.

I learned that it's really easy to go the extra step for someone.

No matter how small, it always makes the difference.

The Oatmeal Man taught me that.

Gary came into the Diner mid-morning one Saturday and was sat in my section. He was there alone. He ordered a cup of coffee and a bowl of oatmeal with brown sugar and raisins. I was cordial with him, kept his coffee full, and wished him a good day as he left.

The following weekend he returned and, by chance, was sat in my section again.

Recognizing him, I greeted him at his table, where again, he was dining alone, and had a coffee for him already in hand. I said, "Good morning, nice to see you again. Here's your coffee. Would you like me to put in your order for your oatmeal with brown sugar and raisins?"

He looked up at me and smiled in disbelief.

And that's when Gary became The Oatmeal Man to me.

Every Saturday after that Gary stopped by the Diner for his coffee and oatmeal and to have a chat. I learned he was an accounting professor at Lehigh University and an avid reader, walker, and golfer. He and his wife were extremely proud of their two sons and he was planning on retiring from teaching and tackling the really long list of books he'd always wanted to read. First up on the list were *The Adventures of Tom Sawyer*, *The Count of Monte Cristo*, and *Oliver Twist*.

It didn't matter how busy I was, I'd always take a few minutes to sit down with Gary at his table and chat with him about what we'd both been up to that week. We talked about everything and loved catching up about what was going on in each other's families.

I relied on him for advice about school, finances, college, and my career.

My college essay in my application to Temple was about The Oatmeal Man and the impact the experience of knowing him had on me.

He got me a book and wrote an incredibly nice note in the cover for my graduation present when I left for college. A fitting gift.

He'd met my parents and had breakfast with them on more than one occasion. And when I left for college, we kept in touch via email. I'd send him a note to let him know when I'd be back in town from school and he'd come by the Diner during my shift to catch up.

On the day of my Air Force commissioning ceremony, he and his wife walked into the St. Joseph's University chapel dressed to the nines, arm in arm, with the biggest smiles on their faces.

I'll never forget the tears streaming down his face when he hugged me and congratulated me endlessly on that really important day of becoming an Air Force officer.

We still keep in touch to this day, well over a decade later. He signs off his emails with, "Still eating oatmeal."

Gary is my frame of reference for the undeniable fact that one tiny extra step—one bowl of oatmeal—can make all the difference.

Every time I'm back in Allentown I always make a stop at Chris'. I don't even have to let them know I'm coming because, for the most part, all the regulars are still there, and I always run into so many of my customers.

I typically have to carve out time to go back there because I end up staying for several hours catching up with everyone.

And I always leave with a full and happy heart and a reminder of all the things I've learned from the best waitressing job in the world.

I spent nine years serving thousands of people their eggs and bacon and toast and coffee.

But the people who touched my life along the way served me something more than any tip—big or small—ever could.

# Revelation 16:

## *Stay in the moment.*
## *Stay in the day.*

Young souls learn to accept responsibility for their actions.
Mature souls learn to accept responsibility for their thoughts.
And old souls learn to accept responsibility for their happiness.

Weeeeeeee,
The Universe

My mom ruined drinking for me.

When she shares her story in meetings, she starts by saying, "It wasn't my worst drink, it was just my last."

I started drinking early on in high school and spent a lot of years questioning whether I'd ever be able to drink like a normal person or if it ran in my blood that I'd be an alcoholic, too.

So I used to joke, "Hi, my name is Sarah and I have a genetic predisposition to maybe, potentially, one day be an alcoholic."

But really, this was always a concern for me.

Any time I drank too much, any time I blacked out, any time I did something stupid while drinking, the regret was an overwhelming feeling and it would take me days—both mentally and physically—to recover from the anxiety that drinking caused.

As I trained for my first figure competition in 2013, I gave up alcohol entirely for the nine months that I trained for the show. It felt incredible. Post competition—I slowly went back to my old habits.

In December 2015, I decided to give up drinking for a year, just to see what my life would be like without alcohol.

I spent the first month in a deep depression, wondering if I'd ever truly have fun being sober. I hated who I was when I was drinking, but I worried that I'd never relate to anyone if I gave it up for good.

I continued my sober year past the one-year mark and had my first drink on New Year's Eve of 2016. I drank on a few occasions into 2017 until February when I decided I like my life better sober.

Like my mom tells in her story, it wasn't my worst drink, either, it just happens to have been my last.

If I look back on my life, every regret or cringe-worthy moment I've ever had has to do with drinking.

I'd gotten to a point where I'd have a bottle of wine to myself at a friend's house and hop in the car and drive myself home.

And the next morning I'd lay in bed with a terrible feeling in the pit of my stomach when I'd think about everything I have to lose—everything I've worked for, all the relationships I care about, and the military and entrepreneurial careers I've built.

Was I willing to throw that away if I got in a car one night and heaven forbid killed someone or myself?

Giving up drinking was the easy part. Continuing to drink the way that I did was something I decided I'd had enough of.

It's easy for me to give it up because I'm as stubborn as they come.

But perhaps it's also been easy because I don't have cravings to drink. I don't struggle with *not* drinking. But I know that once I pick up one drink, all bets are off.

And when it came to a night of drinking, the thought process went like this: Ok, I'll have just this one. When that felt good, I'd order a second, and after the third—because I'm such a lightweight—no good decisions were made. I'd put myself in a position where I'd lost the ability to make the choices I'd make for myself if I weren't drinking.

And so for me, it's easier to just let it go.

What I always found so strange about drinking is I'd ask my friends the next day after a raging night of partying, "Do you feel guilty that we drank so much last night and acted like idiots?" And they'd say, "Hah! No, I had such a blast!"

But for me, I'd literally spend three days trying to get over the guilt of wishing I hadn't drank so much or wondering what I'd said to people or if I acted in a way that, had I been sober, would've been embarrassing.

When I was growing up and I'd do something stupid, I'd consult with my mom and say, "I have one of those pit-of-my-stomach icky feelings about this...," and when it came to drinking, that icky feeling never really went away for me.

So I had a good run of about 15 years, but I'm confident enough today to know that I can have decades upon decades of a full life without the regret that drinking causes for me.

I look back now and think about Major Mac and the second chance that I was given.

The crazy thing about giving up alcohol was that I felt like I was the only one. I'm certainly one of the only people in my immediate circles who chooses not to drink, but once I decided to give it up, I started coming across all of these people on social media and through podcasts and websites and in online communities.

Even though it felt lonely, now I know I'm not the only one. There are people all over the world who've quit drinking or simply choose not to.

This gave me the strength to give it up the way I wanted to—knowing that there are so many other people out there like me who understand that they're simply a better person when alcohol is not involved.

Sometimes, we just need to find the strength to do what's best for ourselves, and it only comes when either the pain is too great to endure or, as I've mentioned before—enough is enough.

While living one day at a time has never been easy for me, my mom reminds me to, "Stay in the moment. Stay in the day."

"There's no fear in the moment," she says.

I don't proclaim that I'll give up drinking for the rest of my life, and even after 23 years of sobriety, my mom doesn't either. You may remember, as she describes it, she's recovering...not recovered.

For me, I just know that for today, I'll decide not to drink.

I never shared publicly my decision to give up drinking until I started writing this book. It was then that I found the courage to speak up in those online communities I'm part of and share my story.

As with my eating disorder, and my battle with anxiety and depression, I think that by opening up about the things we struggle with we can make space for others to open up and find healing, too.

If you happen to be someone struggling with alcohol or addiction and have thought about or wanted to give it up but you weren't quite sure how, the best way to begin is to take it one step at a time.

And never underestimate the power of asking for help.

I try to live in the moment and stay in the day, and when I struggle, I recite the Serenity Prayer that I've said so many times in the rooms of AA, holding hands with and surrounded by recovering alcoholics:

God,
Grant me the serenity,
To accept the things I cannot change,
The courage to change the things I can,
And the wisdom to know the difference.

# Revelation 17:

## *But what if it could be better than you thought?*

When driving down the road of life, rarely do you know how
good you have it, until you see it in the rear-view mirror.
Which is not to suggest that you should look back now,
but to remind you that where you are today is more
awesome and amazing than you probably realize.

10-4,
The Universe

When you're broke in college, studying abroad isn't really an option.

But because Jaclyn and I had full-tuition scholarships as ROTC cadets, we had the opportunity to spend one semester abroad.

It was the definition of a once-in-a-lifetime opportunity.

We landed at Leonardo da Vinci International Airport for what was the beginning of our four-month semester together in Rome.

Our eyes lit up and we giggled and pointed as our shuttle breezed by the Roman Wall and the Colosseum, finally taking us to the beautiful apartment I had been arranging online for the past four months.

It was exactly as it appeared in the pictures from outside. A gorgeous white stone building with big, beautiful windows. We couldn't wait to get inside and see the bright, airy home we were about to have.

We buzzed in at the door, and out of 14 apartments in the building only a few people answered, and not one person knew the name of the man we were trying to reach.

The man we were renting the apartment from was an entrepreneur, and he was working in China selling fine Italian wines, which is why his place was available to us.

When he mailed the keys to us, they didn't arrive in time, so he arranged for his cousin who lived in Rome to be at the apartment with his spare set of keys, waiting for us to arrive.

So why did no one in his building know of him?

Thankfully, we'd met a girl in the airport who was also in our study abroad program and her hotel was just around the corner. She let us keep our eight bags of luggage with her while we sorted things out.

Hours passed, and I started getting a sinking feeling about the whole thing.

Here we were in a city we'd never been to, not knowing a word of Italian, with no means of a phone or internet, and no clue where in the city we were.

We managed to find an Apple store and asked to use one of the model computers for the internet.

We first contacted the guy we were renting from to ask what was up.

I'll back-track to fill you in:

I found the apartment on Craigslist four months prior to going abroad and exchanged weekly e-mail and phone conversations with the man we were renting from.

When we talked on the phone he told me about his life, his job, asked me things about mine, was interested in our studies and travel abroad, and genuinely was a nice person. He had a lovely Italian accent and from the way he spoke about the apartment, we knew our time abroad would be perfect.

When it came time to pay him, he asked that I wire the money to him in China, which I still wasn't comfortable with, even though I felt like I could trust him. I'd consulted with my dad through the entire process of renting this place, and we agreed it'd be best to pay through PayPal.

That was difficult for him to do being in China because of government restrictions…totally legit.

So he asked us to send the money through PayPal to the e-mail address of his sister-in-law, and when we sent her the $1500, she originally sent it back because our guy hadn't yet told her she'd be receiving money…still believable.

We were refunded the money on PayPal and sent it back again.

The money was paid and the keys were on their way and in the days leading up to the trip the man reassured us that we'd be able to get into the place.

So why were we walking around Rome as two homeless foreigners with no apartment?

We promptly received an e-mail back from the sister-in-law who sounded confused and had her whole story mixed up.

She was so surprised that we actually were two sisters currently in Rome who really were expecting to move into an apartment for four months.

And this is when the real story came out.

The woman provided us with a phone number that was supposed to be for the cousin who was to meet us at the apartment.

The number appeared to be for a phone in Denmark, not Italy, and we later learned that those digits were actually a tracking number to a FedEx package.

This woman was not actually this man's sister-in-law. Rather, she was an American who thought she was dating a man living in China who she met over the internet, but had not met in person.

He had been sending her e-mails and messages to wire $1500 for his friend (the "cousin") to purchase three computers and have them sent to China.

Hence the reason the woman originally sent the money back to us—she was told she'd receive money intended for the purchase of computers, and couldn't understand why some strange girl was talking about an apartment in Italy.

It was official. We were scammed, and so was she.

I literally thought this was something that only happens to people who appear on "Dr. Phil." And now here we were in the middle of some crazy Craigslist scam.

We forwarded all contact with these two people to my dad, who passed it to the FBI to investigate the case.

But we were going to have to move on. We needed a place to live.

We found a hostel to stay the night, just up the street from the Colosseum.

The place was relatively nice, the owners were great to us, and we quickly made a few friends.

It didn't make sense to sit around and pout. Things had to work out one way or another.

We went out and walked around the city and sat at a café and drank Peronis and stopped at a pizzeria to have our first pizza in Rome. We laughed all night and took pictures and made some wonderful memories with our new British friends we'd met in the hostel.

Our first day in Rome felt like an eternity and we slept heavy that night from the weight of it all.

The next day we woke up early, booked another night at the hostel for good measure, and walked a little over two miles to the Temple Rome campus.

There, the staff had already received word of our situation from the e-mail we sent the day before.

They felt so sorry for us and made it clear that they would do anything in their power to help. We were grateful, because we'd elected not to stay in campus-affiliated housing so that we could have an authentic experience.

They recommended several options of apartments to us and gave us different suggestions on how to go about finding a place. So we felt like we at least had options.

They put in a few calls for us and we decided to explore some sites while we were waiting to hear news of potential apartments.

We walked to see the Piazza del Popolo, the Piazza di Spagna, and the Villa Borghese.

Hours later we got back to the campus and had received a tip for an apartment.

One of the faculty members called the woman and, in Italian, arranged for us to see her apartment. She gushed that it was just a ten-minute walk from the campus and was so excited for us.

As we walked, I told Jaclyn not to expect anything great so as not to be disappointed if the place was awful.

We got to the door and I rang the buzzer. In English, a man said, "Come up, it's on the top floor."

We giggled the whole way up to the eighth floor in the creaky elevator, to be greeted by a man, the woman's son.

When we walked into the apartment, it led straight to the most beautiful terrace I've ever stood on.

Next we were shown the living room and dining room, where a hallway led to a completely separate apartment.

Another hallway led to the bathroom and the kitchen and yet another hallway led to two beautiful bedrooms.

This place was absolutely amazing and we probably couldn't afford it.

After being shown the apartment and chatting with the woman and her son, we discussed rent.

Five hundred and fifty Euro a month for one person, and they'd make it 800 Euro for the two of us. We'd each have our own bedrooms, and it was going to be cheaper than the place we'd been scammed out of.

We both already knew which rooms we wanted. My sister wanted the bright cheery room with the large windows and I wanted the room that had tons of light and big double doors that opened to the terrace.

We told her we'd take it, and she told us we could move in first thing in the morning.

We didn't take for granted one day we got to sit out on that terrace watching the sun set on the Vatican and soaking it all in.

"SUCH IS LIFE," we hollered and laughed so many times while we'd sit there and recall that awful moment of realizing we'd been scammed.

But we truly felt like this had happened to us for a reason.

We loved where we lived and the wonderful woman we lived with and her son.

We learned so much from her, as she's a well-known author, artist, and director. Her husband was an American who served in the Army and was a journalist with Variety magazine. Her son is a famous Italian composer, and her daughter is an actress and at the time was living in New York City.

So while the apartment was incredible and the view was one I'll never forget, our experience was even better because of this family that opened their home to us for that truly Italian experience we'd hoped for.

We trekked to every single part of Rome possible in the months we lived there, and on the weekends, we managed to travel to Venice, Pordenone, Florence, Munich, Barcelona, Dublin, London, Paris, Athens, Brussels, and Bruges.

On that first day in Rome, it felt like the next four months were going to be impossible to enjoy with such a heavy disappointment. I was worried that Jackie wouldn't trust me and that I'd let her down.

On the very last day we spent in Rome we'd saved the Colosseum and going to the top of the Vatican for last. We wanted to leave the city with the best view there is.

So while we walked around and got our last cappuccinos, last piece of pizza, and had our last glass of wine, we were walking down the street when we realized exactly where we were— standing right in front of the apartment building that was supposed to have been our home.

Everything came full circle.

The case was never closed on the man who scammed us and we never got our money back.

But the semester we spent abroad were four of the best months of our lives.

I guess, sometimes in life, things turn out better than you could ever expect.

# Revelation 18:

## *Life's hard.*
## *Pray harder.*

Adversity, challenges, and bumps in the road, are often
the first signs that a great healing has begun.

Thinking of you,
The Universe

Even before I began planning the chapters for this book, I
knew my grandma, Helen, would have a chapter of her own.

She's taught me one of the very best lessons in life:

Life's hard. Pray harder.

She's been my only living grandparent for most of my life. My
grandpa—her husband—passed away several months after I
was born, and my grandparents on my dad's side both passed
away when I was still a kid. While I have memories of the two
of them, they're vague.

So I'm extremely lucky at 30 years old to have her here. But as
I sat down to draft this chapter, I realized there was still so
little I actually knew about her life before I was ever in it. In
order to tell this story properly, I realized there was so much
more I wanted to know.

She lived in York, Pennsylvania most of my childhood and
moved to Florida almost 20 years ago. So we've only ever had
the opportunity to see each other during holidays or if I'd
travel to Florida with my mom on vacation.

Helen Finney is the godliest woman there is. And she's one hell of a hard worker—even at 83 years old. I admire her work ethic and dedication to her faith as the years pass, especially as she gets older and that faith seemingly gets stronger.

But I wondered what made her that way?

In the process of writing this book I went to Florida so that we could sit down and talk, and I could finally learn all the things about her that I never knew, simply because I never took the time to stop and ask.

I was disappointed in myself for going all these years without really getting to know and develop a relationship with my only grandparent. But I'm extremely grateful to have recognized it in time to make that right.

So one afternoon during the trip I grabbed my laptop and we both went into her bedroom. She sat in her favorite recliner with her feet up and the TV, turned to HGTV, on mute.

I stacked a few pillows at the foot of the bed and laid with my feet at the headboard, my computer in my lap.

And I asked her to start from the beginning.

For several hours we sat together in her room while she told me stories from a long, full, and mostly happy life.

We laughed and carried on and talked about the bad sprinkled among so much good.

I'd never felt so close to my grandma as I did in that moment in time, just the two of us. I know it's something I'll never forget and will cherish that gift for the rest of what I hope will be my long, full, and mostly happy life.

The story I wanted to share is of my grandmother's strength, the work of her life, and the hope she's held in her heart. So let me fill in the details of Helen Finney's life so that her story has more context, like it does now for me.

At 83 years old, she's lived in Pennsylvania and then Florida her whole life and never had the desire to travel or see the world. She didn't intend to go to college and then never decided to. There was never money for any of that.

She's the fourth oldest in a family of eight children—three boys and five girls—and grew up in a three-bedroom, one-bathroom home in the small coal mining town of Saxton, Pennsylvania.

Her father, Clinton, was a coal miner, then sheriff, and then constable of the town, and a kind, caring man. Her mother, Sarah—whose name I carry on—was a school teacher and used sternness to show love for her children.

Helen recalled her childhood as a series of happy memories in a loving family.

After long days at the mine, dad would come home and sit each child on his lap and sing them old folk songs. Mom came home from school to cook and make sure the family was well cared for.

Some nights, they gathered around the piano while mom played, dad sang tenor, and the kids all sang along.

She smiled and laughed as she told me these things and I thought about how our lives have been so completely different.

The world was a very different place to grow up in the 1930s and her small-town suburban childhood sounded a lot like an episode of "The Waltons."

She talked about growing up in a time where the bathroom was an outhouse, going sledding in the winter on a sheet of metal, and helping her mom canning vegetables from their garden. About going to sock hops and listening to the radio as a family to hear about what was happening in the world. One of the biggest events in their home was getting a flushing toilet in the house. I thought about the bathroom saga of a house with 10 people.

She was raised a Christian and their family was in church every Sunday, so from the very beginning she learned to rely on her faith.

While she and her dad got along, she and her mom grew apart as she got older, at odds over her mother's expectations and my grandma's life choices.

At 17 years old, she couldn't wait to get out of that "one-horse town," as she called it, and she and her older sister moved to Harrisburg, Pennsylvania together to live in the "big city." Her words.

They got a small apartment and secretary jobs and double dated, went dancing, and had fun being city girls. One night while out on the town, she met Robert Finney, my grandpa.

He was a handsome man and a Navy medical corpsman in the Korean War. They called him "Doc Finney," and he was on the ship and overseas more than he wasn't.

A year after she met my grandpa, while he was overseas, she found out she was pregnant, and her mother disowned her. She didn't want my grandpa to know and planned to raise her baby on her own, not wanting to have to get married because of the baby. But when my grandpa caught wind of the news from his own mom, he immediately took leave to come home and see his first son.

They were married a few months later and my grandpa ended up having to adopt his own son because his name, as the father, was not on the birth certificate.

By that time my grandma had become a devout Christian and re-dedicated her life to her faith. When her father passed away from a sudden heart attack, she repaired that frayed relationship with her mother and they grew closer in the remaining years of her mom's life—she credits her faith for making that possible.

Robert and Helen settled down in a small house in York, Pennsylvania. My grandpa was stationed in Maryland and was home only on the weekends.

My grandma says she never wanted to have kids, but she and Robert went on to have five more. After her first son, my mom was next, followed by another daughter. Then 13 years later—to everyone's surprise—she had another boy, followed then by fraternal twin boys.

She worked at the local Getty's Pet Shop for 30 years and my grandpa served in the Navy for 23 years until his Diabetes, diagnosed in his teens, was affecting his health and forced him to retire.

It was hard for him to adjust to civilian life and he began drinking to cope.

He'd started a small siding company but paired gambling with his new drinking habit and was never around.

He was unfaithful and began gambling all of their money away, and while he'd give my grandma a small amount of money to buy groceries and pay the bills, the rest went to bars, his girlfriends, and the horse track.

When he stepped on a nail at work one day, it began a 13-year nightmare of gangrene in his legs until he eventually lost both of them, then lost the function of his bowels, lost his sight, and was on dialysis for kidney failure.

Several years after he passed away, my grandma moved to Florida to be closer to her sister. Together, they made their money by cleaning condos at her condominium complex.

Eventually, four of my grandma's six children moved to Florida, too.

She'd been diagnosed with osteoarthritis in her 40s, and as the years have passed, her hands have suffered the worst of it.

Even as she began losing function of her hands, she continued to clean, cooked for her neighbors, and volunteered at church.

She lived alone until turning 80 years old when she moved into an assisted living facility. Five months later she moved in with my mom, instead, where she now keeps busy by reading, taking the dog for a walk, and cleaning the house. She likes to make the beds and vacuum and do the laundry. She loves to sit out on the patio in the shade by the pool.

From the time she was a kid my grandma has worked every day of her life, and she's found ways to work around the limited use of her hands. They've grown knobby and weak over the years, yet she still manicures her own nails and always has a fresh coat of nail polish on them.

I've paid close attention to her hands over the years as I've watched them change while she's aged.

And while she's embarrassed for people to see them, I think they are absolutely beautiful.

Earlier in the year I asked to photograph her hands. She didn't love the idea but went along with it. I took her outside and had her place them on a patio ottoman so I could capture them in detail. I printed and framed this lovely photo of her hands in black and white. It's now one of the most treasured keepsakes I own.

To me, her hands have always been the surest visible sign of what an amazing and hard-working woman she is. Those hands have lovingly cared for one man, raised six children, cared for, cooked for, cleaned for, loved on, and prayed for too many people to count.

They're a sign of strength—not weakness—because they've endured all the things life has put before her.

To me, her hands signify a life well-loved and well-lived.

And when life's been hard, she's folded those hands together and prayed harder.

I asked my grandma for her wisdom. What advice does she have for me to live a full life like hers?

"My dad always said, 'You will always get back what you give. And if you care about people it'll come back to you.'"

She went on,

"My faith has always been part of my life through all the bad and the things that don't let you believe in faith. The things you go through make you stronger, and I think you learn from those things no matter how old you live to be.

"People are fragile and vulnerable, and we can't figure it out like the Lord can. I think the Lord gives you just as much as you can bear—he knows just how much you can handle."

I feel like I try my best to consciously make the most of my life—to seize opportunities, chase my dreams, and live life to the fullest.

It's in my adult life, though, that I've really learned to cherish the relationships we have while we have them—to make the most of the time we're given with the people who hold meaning for us and have a place in our hearts.

I knew I wanted to share something that has been very important to me—my grandma's ability to keep her faith when life has given her plenty of reasons to lose hope.

But in writing this lesson I learned a different, and equally important lesson, one that my grandma has also now taught me:

Make the most of the time you're given...both for yourself and with the people who matter to you.

# Revelation 19:

## *There are no coincidences.*

All that you need, to have what you want,
lies inside of you, right now.

Everything,
The Universe


When Caitlin and I got called down to the guidance counselor's office just after the New Year's holiday break, I had no idea what we could be in trouble for.

She and I sat by each other in homeroom and both Jason, Caitlin, and I spent every morning chatting and goofing around.

Jason never liked to say the "Pledge of Allegiance," so I said it twice as loud for the two of us.

When he and Caitlin started dating, I was so excited for both of them. Caitlin and I had known each other since we were little kids, and Jason had just moved to the school district that year.

It was ninth grade, and we were all navigating our freshman year of high school together.

Caitlin was artsy, Jason was a bit grunge, and I was the co-captain of the cheerleading team. The three of us maybe didn't make sense in the social circles of high school, but in homeroom we were quite the little clique.

So when the guidance counselor told me Jason put a gun to his head and took his own life, I never knew I had the capacity to be so angry at someone.

I didn't know it was possible to feel more mad, than sad, when someone you care about dies.

A few weeks prior, Jason had passed around a note at school.

On it was a list of people's names and a message at the top about making choices. Then there were two columns below: truth or dare. The instruction of the note was, after reading it, to choose either truth or dare, write your choice by your name, and then pass it to a person on the list who hadn't yet picked.

I remember myself hurriedly picking truth and passing the note on, thinking he was just up to some weird Jason thing, which was typical for him.

Was that note supposed to have been a sign?

For years I beat myself up over the fact that I *should've* known.

Why didn't I ask him?

Why didn't I bring it up to Caitlin?

Why didn't I say anything?

I think a part of me felt like it might have been serious, but the bigger part of me chalked it up to it being another Jason-ism and left it at that.

The latter was so much more likely because he was always writing and questioning and doing, and it seemed totally normal that he was just pondering life, as always.

I've asked myself countless times over the years, *How couldn't I have known?* It was so plainly right there in front of me that he needed help.

But looking back, how *could* I have known that's what that note might have been about?

I'm not certain anyone in my circle of friends knew who Jason was, let alone that I was friends with him and was suffering his loss. The entire thing made no sense, and I was not prepared to handle a loss like that, or to watch Caitlin and Jason's closest friends suffer like they did.

So later that year—it happened to be the day of my birthday—Caitlin and I decided to go visit Jason's mom to check in and see how she was doing.

She seemed to be holding it together as best she could and managed to laugh while we told her funny stories and reminisced about her son.

Then she told us a story that was so incredibly Jason—true to form—that it makes me laugh even today to think of it.

Jason really wanted to go to culinary school. It had always been his dream.

But when he asked his mom for a subscription to a culinary magazine for $20, she'd said no.

In true Jason fashion, he'd subscribed anyway, choosing the "Bill me later" option on the mail-in postcard.

After Jason's death, his mom got a bill in the mail for a culinary magazine subscription, and she had a good laugh that her sneaky son had gotten away with it.

She was outside taking care of the lawn one day at their suburban neighborhood home when she looked down at her angel statues in her flowerbeds and couldn't believe what she was seeing.

She bent down to get closer and—sure enough—there was a $20 bill stuck under one of the angel's wings.

She hesitated as she reached out to grab it, as if she was seeing things and it couldn't possibly be real.

Then this grieving mom stood in her yard surrounded by her angels and had a good, long belly laugh. She promptly displayed the bill on her refrigerator and when she showed it to us it was like she was still in disbelief.

*There are no coincidences*, I thought, when she told us this incredible story.

After that visit, while Jason had passed away, I'd been feeling more and more like maybe he never really left.

You might remember the show "Crossing Over" with John Edward from the early 2000s. Or maybe more recently you're familiar with the show "Long Island Medium" with Theresa Caputo.

Either way, my mom has the ability to speak with and through those who've crossed over.

Sometime after Jason had passed, I was at home one night crying about a boy who dumped me.

I was supposed to go to this party because he was going to be there and I thought it'd be my chance to see him, but I couldn't find the phone number of the person I needed to reach in order to go.

The phone number was written down on a piece of paper, and I looked everywhere for it and worked myself up into a meltdown when I searched all over the house but couldn't find it.

My mom had thought I'd carried on long enough. And when she came to the living room to talk some sense into me, she caught me totally by surprise.

"Sarah, Jason's *here*," she said to me from the kitchen as I was sitting in the living room at our family computer desk.

I was surprised to hear her say his name, and immediately mad at her for bringing him up.

Her encounters with perfect strangers when someone who has passed has a message to deliver to someone living were never off before. But I wondered if she was making this up just simply to make me feel better.

She said a few things that sounded just like motherly advice, but then she talked about how Jason was disappointed I was sitting around wasting time being sad about something so trivial, when he didn't even have a chance anymore to keep living. She also said that he was sorry for what he'd done and for the way he left all of us.

And then she *did* something that almost knocked me off my chair.

"He's about to go," she said. "But before he does he wants me to do this one thing, what does *this* mean to you?"

She made a tapping motion with her right pointer finger, as if to mimic tapping someone on the shoulder.

*There are no coincidences.*

I knew it was Jason.

We were in several classes together throughout the day, one of them was Spanish.

In most of our classes together, the teachers sat the students side by side in alphabetical order, but in Spanish class there were single-file rows that snaked alphabetically throughout the classroom.

So in Spanish class, Jason sat directly behind me.

And I used to get in trouble daily by Senora for turning around to talk to Jason after he'd tap me on my right shoulder with the eraser-side of his pencil to get my attention.

Senora would say, "Sarina," Spanish for "Little Sarah" to get me to turn back around and pay attention. I was always aggravated with him for constantly getting me in trouble for talking in class.

Nobody would know that aside from Jason, Senora, and me. Perhaps a few of the kids in the class, but certainly not my mom.

I was frozen after she'd made this gesture and had no idea what to think.

"One last thing, he says," my mom added. "The paper is on your desk in your room right where you'd left it.

"Go upstairs and look," she nudged.

And sure enough, it was there on my desk mixed in with a few other things. I'd looked in that exact place what seemed to be a hundred times before, but there it was.

And like Jason's mom, I stood there in my room and had a good, long belly laugh. But instead of displaying this paper on the fridge, I crumpled it up and threw it away, and I never did try to see that boy again.

A friend of mine whose mom also had this "gift" to speak with those who've crossed over, said that if I pay attention and really listen, that I'll be able to feel and know that I have this gift, too, as she's learned that she does.

I've never *talked* with Jason or *heard* from him or anyone else that has passed, that I know of.

Yet I fully believe today, that while he's gone, he never really left.

While I haven't *heard* from him myself, sometimes I think maybe I'm not yet supposed to.

I could tell you stories upon stories about my mom and her encounters with passing information to strangers from those who've passed away.

Perhaps we'll save that for the next book.

And so while I can't explain it—and while all logic tells us it's impossible or untrue—I continue to believe that there are no coincidences.

After all, I did choose truth.

# Revelation 20:

## *You don't have to know what you want for the rest of your life but you do have to be prepared, so that when the moment presents itself, you're ready.*

Dreams come true, that's what they do. The only variable is when. For the slow approach: Resist. Attach. Insist. Deny. Stop. Second guess. Whine. Argue. Defend. Protest. Cry. Struggle. And ask others, when you know the answer yourself. For the quick approach: Visualize. Pretend. Prepare. Dodge. Roll. Serpentine. Do not waiver over intentions, but over methods. Show up, even when nothing happens. And give thanks in advance.

You knew that,
The Universe

The title of this chapter are words Chris said to me while we were sitting at work one day.

He'll tell you he doesn't remember saying something he agrees is pretty profound, but he also believes wholeheartedly in that advice.

I'm so thankful I took it literally.

When I committed to Air Force ROTC I knew that I'd have a four-year commitment to serve on active duty following college.

I was 20 years old when I joined ROTC and 24 years old when I arrived on Guam in December 2011 for my first day of active duty. This would've made me almost 28 years old when I'd first have a chance to get out of the Air Force.

I remember when I was signing my scholarship paperwork how far away that felt.

Through a program called Tuition Assistance, the Air Force pays for a portion of a degree while you're on active duty, and will also pay for one certification.

So the advice you're given as a young officer is to get your master's degree out of the way as quickly as you can. Not only because you gain more responsibility—and thus less free time—as you gain more rank and it helped you qualify for better positions, but because at the time government funding for TA was drying up and there was talk that it would disappear completely.

Signing up for my master's degree meant that I'd be adding time to my initial four-year commitment, as you can sometimes owe extra time in service if the time in which you receive funding for your education extends past your original service commitment.

The concept can be quite confusing, but the point in mentioning it is that I was pressured to make a decision about my master's program because I didn't want to accrue an additional commitment to active duty that I wasn't sure at the time I was ready to take on.

Fortunately my master's degree was a one-year intensive program and only added six months extra to my four-year commitment. With the help of the TA program, I was able to pay for the degree in full without needing loans or going into any debt. I also took advantage of the certificate option to acquire my nutrition specialist certification.

In addition to taking care of my secondary education, I put myself on a really aggressive payment plan to pay off all of my student loans.

While I was on a full scholarship with a stipend for living expenses in ROTC, I still accepted the student loans I'd originally applied for so that I had extra money on top of my part-time jobs.

I consolidated those loans for a lower interest rate and paid it off in three years as opposed to ten. This meant I was mostly broke for my first several years in the Air Force, with having to pay rent, bills, living expenses, and paying off my student debt. I also had money deducted from my paycheck for long-term investments.

So while I was making great money in my first several years on active duty, I lived like I only had a few hundred dollars to my name.

I bought a cheap car on Guam, my little "Guam Bomb," as we called them, with cash and sold it when I left.

I used that money as a down payment on a brand-new car when I moved back to the States and paid off the balance in three years to boost my credit and so that I'd own it outright.

I was smart about how much leave (paid time off) I used over the years, knowing that if I was planning to separate from active duty, that I'd want to have terminal leave—essentially a bunch of saved up, unused days off—that I'd saved and could take advantage of and still get paid while in the process of transitioning to whatever came next.

I spent a total of six and a half years on active duty as a public affairs officer, learning anything and everything you could ever want to know about communications, media, strategy, planning, running a newspaper, overseeing a website, managing a large team, working for the equivalent of an executive, hiring, firing, mentoring, budgeting, leadership, and more.

My experiences in the Air Force have prepared me for so many opportunities, whether I choose to work for myself or for someone else throughout the rest of my life.

I was never taught how to manage money growing up. And back in college during some of those really desperate times, I worried that I was destined to struggle with money for the rest of my life—that I'd never have any sense of stability or peace of mind when it came to my finances.

So it's not that I had some master plan or knew all the right steps to take, but every paycheck that came my way, I just did the next right thing with the money.

I've paid off every cent of debt to my name and made massive investments in my future in terms of education, learning how best to manage funds, and investing money.

I'd also built a business that, while it was a small, side-hustle hobby leading up to the time that I was ready to transition, had the foundation to be a massive success.

It would've been easier to take another assignment and spend at least another two-to-three years on active duty.

I would've been able to put away a lot more money, I could've grown my business to a stable and comfortable place, and I may have had a more concrete idea of what I wanted my future to look like.

As far as my career was concerned, before I dove into personal training I thought I'd stay on active duty until retirement because I had no other plan.

But from the moment I dove into training for that first figure competition, to coaching my very first personal training client, I knew I wasn't going to stay on active duty forever.

My mindset at the time was that I'd stay in the Air Force so long as I was having fun. I'd taken an oath and I took my responsibilities seriously, but in the back of my mind I always approached my career from two fronts: *plan as if you're going to be in the Air Force for the long haul, and also like you'd be ready to get out tomorrow.*

Chris' advice motivated me to take care of my finances and my career so that I'd always have the freedom to choose what came next for me.

So when the opportunities I was given for a next assignment didn't jibe with what I wanted next for me, I was ready.

And the opportunity to continue to serve as an Air Force Reservist so I can run my business full time, couldn't be a more perfect way for me to press on with creating a life of my dreams.

I still get to serve one weekend every month and two weeks per year, wear my uniform, and be part of the Air Force family that I love so much.

But now I get to play full out with my business without holding back. I have the time, the footing, and the support to dedicate everything I have to the one thing I've been dreaming of my whole life: helping others.

Back when I was handed my uniforms and called Cadet Bergstein I had no idea what the Air Force would have in store for me, or that along the way I'd learn so much, be given so much opportunity and responsibility, and that it would give me the stability I craved so badly when things were hard in college.

While Chris might not remember what he said that day in the office, I know it's something I won't ever forget.

You don't have to know what you want for the rest of your life but you do have to be prepared, so that when the moment presents itself, you're ready.

And man, am I ready.

# Revelation 21:

## *You already are successful...don't miss it.*

Until the really "great" stuff comes along, do the
not-so-great stuff. The not-so-great stuff always leads
to the great stuff. Whereas doing nothing pretty
much leads to nowhere. And do it with a passion.

Tallyho,
The Universe

It was my first public failure as a business owner. Except that no one else noticed it.

I'd spent an entire month creating a new workout and nutrition program that I was planning to sell to my small online audience.

I created the program essentially in secret, not wanting to reveal too much about it in case I couldn't actually get it done in time.

So when I was ready to launch it to the world I'd been talking about it publicly for just a few weeks in sporadic social media posts.

I knew what it took to market a program, to build an audience, and to attract hundreds, if not thousands, of people.

I'd spent several months working with a business coach who walked me through the steps a number of times, and I have a ton of friends in the industry, plus endless amounts of personal knowledge from my own research, job experience, and professional development.

It wasn't that I didn't have the knowledge, resources, or couldn't ask for help along the way. But I had every excuse for taking the shortcut.

I wasn't scared that the program would fail, because I knew I had built a great program. But as I was creating it, I nitpicked every detail and sabotaged my potential success at every step along the way.

I didn't have money to pay a team. I didn't have a whole lot of time on my hands because of my full-time Air Force job. I had a small audience. Nobody knew what I was working on, so nobody could really care what I was working on.

I could go on and on.

I was plagued with limiting beliefs and had every excuse you could think of.

So the night before the program launched I stayed up late making sure every last piece of my website was in place for all the sales that would be rolling in come morning.

I woke up super early and launched the program and felt a tremendous amount of excitement and stress.

I'd taken the day off of work so that I could celebrate the success of the launch with my mom.

While I was fully expecting orders to be flying in all day long, I was also worried that my site would crash due to all the activity.

By 5 p.m. that day, I had exactly *one* order of the program and it was from my Dad, who'd snuck upstairs while I was crying in my parents' kitchen and purchased the program just so I'd officially have one sale.

I felt like a complete and utter failure. How could I possibly be so bad at being an entrepreneur that nobody—not one of the almost 10,000 people who follow me online—wanted to buy this incredible program that I worked so hard to create and would genuinely help people?

I thought about quitting my business that very day. This was before I'd spoken to the person that would dictate my next Air Force assignment.

In that moment, I was ready to give up on my dreams and just stay on active duty for another three years—or maybe even until I reached the full 20 years of service so I could collect retirement.

My Air Force job was easy enough. It was stressful at times, but not to the point of causing me mental or physical breakdowns. It was fun and exciting and challenging, and I made really good money and had great benefits.

As my mind raced through all these life decisions I was just overwhelmingly sad about the fact that I'd failed in such a huge way. It's really easy to get wrapped up in the embarrassment and overreact to the ego hit we experience when things don't go our way.

Several days later on the phone with my mom, I was still the host—and only guest—of my very own pity party.

Couldn't even get anyone else to attend that one, either.

I knew my parents felt really sad for me and were doing the best they could to keep my spirits up after having been through such a huge disappointment. But there always comes *that* time for my mom when enough is enough, and as she'd say, "All you get from sitting on the pity pot is a big red ring around your ass."

So in the middle of complaining to her about all the reasons why I was never going to make it as a successful entrepreneur she cut me off and said, "You know what, Sarah, you already *are* successful, but you are missing it completely."

She listed off the things I'd done in the past decade before arriving at this less-than-glorious moment in my business:

"You made it through college when the odds were against you. Then you earned a scholarship and studied abroad in Rome. You joined the Air Force and became an officer and lived on Guam and have traveled the world. You've competed in a bodybuilding competition and turned your health around and got your master's degree and coaching certifications so that you could help other people. You run an office of people and work for the most important person on your base and you have done so much. In addition to that you've started a business *while* having a full-time career and an obligation to the Air Force.

"Don't let this one little moment negate all the things you've done to get to this point," she said.

"You haven't actually failed yet, you're just getting started and you just haven't gotten it quite right yet."

And in true mom fashion, she said it again just to make sure it hit home:

"You already *are* successful, Sarah. But you're missing it completely."

That "failure" is hilarious to look back on now because I hardly failed at all. I spent a month creating something I'd envisioned and made it a reality. I positioned it poorly and marketed it even worse, and because of that, the program didn't do well. I didn't lose money, nothing was broken, and no lives were lost in the process.

Aside from the swift kick to my ego, I hadn't actually failed, but I did have the opportunity to understand and be reminded that not everything will go your way in business—or in life—especially not the first time around.

Better still?

I have a solid program now on hand that can be revamped and repositioned to be made wildly successful and help more people than I could even imagine. And I have a whole host of lessons learned from making all the mistakes the first time around.

We tend to look outside ourselves for answers, but oftentimes—like Dadaji and learning to meditate taught me—all the tools and everything we could ever need to succeed in absolutely anything in life is already within us.

But we have to be paying attention to it.

Are you paying attention?

One of the reasons I love the life of entrepreneurship is because of a question Chris asked me several years ago when I was first thinking about running a business but afraid to actually take the leap from the Air Force.

He said, "What's the absolute worst-case scenario that could happen? Even if you failed, lost all your money, and messed it all up, you'd still have your life and the ability to start over again. So if that's the *worst case*, why not go for it?"

He's absolutely right.

Might as well go for it. What's the worst that could happen?

# Revelation 22:

## *Live in the solution,*
## *not the problem.*

It's supposed to be easy. Everything is supposed to be easy.
Everything is easy. You live in a dream world. You're
surrounded by illusions. And the illusions change when
you change your thinking! Tell yourself it's easy. Tell
yourself often. Make it an affirmation. Eat, sleep, breathe
it, and your life shall be transformed.

It's supposed to be easy,
The Universe

She saw three green lights coming her way, so she shined her flashlight to make herself known. While she expected them to go right or left, the boat wasn't slowing down.

Christy will tell you the first miracle was that something—an angel, she believes—helped to orient her after being struck by the boat in the shoulder. It gave her the mind in that split second to use the bottom of the boat to push away down into the water so as not to be struck by the propeller.

She was visiting friends in Destin, Florida and was paddle boarding at night in a protected cove right behind her friend's house. She'd done this dozens of times before.

Her boyfriend at the time, Tim, rushed to her and made a tourniquet out of his shirt to help stop the bleeding.

Her leg was hanging on by the hamstring muscle as the propeller had severed through bone, cartilage, and the femoral artery.

You can bleed out of your femoral artery in three-to-five minutes and when Christy arrived at the hospital her hemoglobin level was at six. The normal range is between 12 and 15 and death is imminent at level four.

Tim said he heard her call out, "Help me, Jesus," in the water and while she could tell this was serious, she was seemingly calm during the whole incident. Her mind flashed to work and how they'd probably have to take her off the schedule for quite some time.

Christy was the graduation speaker of my Air Force Squadron Officer School in early 2016. We'd never met and I wasn't familiar with her story, but I found myself in tears as she stood before her classmates and peers—600 Air Force captains—and spoke to us about what it means to carry on in spite of life's challenges.

I never told her this, but I sat there feeling almost envious of her.

It was the weirdest emotion to have. How could I envy someone who would've never chosen to bear such an incredible burden?

While it felt wrong to feel that way, I understood the place it was coming from. She'd taken a horrible situation and turned it into something incredible.

That's exactly what I'd been trying to do with my life, and from the time I was a young girl I dreamed of a life of helping others.

It's why I loved waitressing at Chris' Diner. It's the true reason I wanted to become a brain surgeon. It's why I wanted to be the Mayor of Philadelphia, and a piece of why I joined the military. And it's absolutely why I became a personal trainer, nutrition specialist, and life coach.

What initially felt like envy, I later realized was genuine admiration for Christy because of all that she endured.

She inspired me in a big way by taking this accident and using it in a positive way to help so many people.

When I sat down to decide on the most important lessons I'd include in this book, I knew I had to share Christy's story—because she is someone who inspired me to finally share mine.

I always think of her now when this lesson comes up for me that my mom taught me years ago:

*Live in the solution, not the problem.*

Being a doer was in Christy's blood.

Before the accident she was involved in every activity under the sun and always found herself busy living life to the fullest.

She graduated from the Air Force Academy in 2009 and went on to become an HC-130J Combat Search and Rescue pilot. In other words, she flies the planes that pararescuers jump out of the back of, and is the same aircraft that refuels helicopters.

It never occurred to her that she wouldn't go back to flying.

Her goal was to be in and out of the The Center for the Intrepid of the San Antonio Military Medical Center in Texas in a few months and back to flying that fall.

While her outlook and determination following the hit-and-run accident was positive, her chances of flying again were looking slim, as she had to work through two different and very strict medical boards in order to become qualified to fly all over again.

Christy is the sixth Air Force amputee pilot to return to service. Within just weeks of the accident, all five fellow amputee pilots had called her or reached out in some way to offer their love, support, and advice.

She told me their support made it easy for her not to despair, because she never had to doubt whether or not she could actually do the hard things—like return to flying.

She and her twin sister, Jessica, joke that the miracles started in the water the night of the accident and they just haven't stopped since.

Jessica was a medical student awaiting residency acceptance and assisting with the nonprofit Children of the Nations in her free time. Her only experience with amputees was in the aftermath of the 2010 earthquake in Haiti.

Through her experience with both Dominican and Haitian populations, she'd been exposed to an ongoing problem regarding the need for prosthetic limbs for children, as young amputees continue to grow out of their preliminary devices.

In these regions, many families simply can't afford the ongoing costs for prosthetics.

Jessica and Christy were so overwhelmed with love following the accident.

It was in the hospital, in fact, that Christy's boyfriend said they needed to turn this life-changing event and the support they'd received into something positive to help others.

And with that spirit, they put together their first event, a paddle board race at the site of the accident to raise money for children in need of prosthetics.

An entire community rallied behind them. Three months after her accident 80 people registered for the race and helped raise $5,000 for their newly-formed foundation, One Leg Up on Life.

To date, OLUOL has raised more than $50,000 and provided care for more than 50 patients, including fitting more than 30 prosthetic limbs for children in need.

In the rehab center at the beginning of her recovery, a fellow amputee said to Christy something she'd never forget:

"Don't for one second long for what you were, but recklessly pursue what you can become."

Being the doer she is, Christy didn't waste even one second.

In fact, just two months after the accident, while recovering—and in addition to forming their nonprofit—she competed in the 2015 Warrior Games at Marine Corps Base Quantico in Virginia.

She came away with 11 medals.

In 2016 she competed in the Invictus Games in Orlando, Florida in the categories of track and field, swimming, rowing, and cycling.

In June of that year Captain Christy Wise followed the path of the other five amputee pilots and became the first Air Force female amputee to return to flying duty.

She maintains her full flying status to this day.

Whenever I think of my problems or limitations, I think about how Christy sees opportunities and possibilities.

Today, Christy is flying, training, following her dream of fostering children, and enjoying her life to the fullest.

She's dedicated herself to a life of service, both to her nation, and to those in need.

Christy may have lost her leg, but she'll never lose her spirit.

She chooses, each and every day, to live in the solution, and recklessly pursues all that her life has and can become.

# Revelation 23:

*I have everything I could ever want,
it just looks different than I thought.*

A tip on legend making: Instead of waiting
for something better, create it.

Keep the change,
The Universe

I hated coming home to an empty house.

Chris and I lived in different cities from the time we started dating. While I never liked having roommates, I still hated coming home to my empty apartment after a long day or after having spent a weekend with Chris or family or friends.

My girlfriend and I decided one weeknight to go to dinner at a place we'd never been to and take a yoga class at a private studio we never tried in a town neither of us had ever been to.

The restaurant was great and we enjoyed our meal, and in between dinner and the class we had time to kill, so as we drove around this tiny little Delaware town I spotted a pet store and wanted to stop in.

Remember Bruno, the rabbit I had in college?

He was the sweetest pet. All my high school and college friends knew him and loved him and no one could believe his personality—he was just like both a dog and a cat. He lived seven long, full, happy, floppy-eared years, and I grieved his loss for a very long time. He was so special and, like everyone said, there was just something about him. I was certain I'd never have another pet like him.

But I'd been thinking about and warming up to the idea of taking the leap and getting another bunny. I'd been feeling like I was ready for the possibility of a new pet. And I figured if we stopped in the store we could look and see if they had any.

The store turned out to be a pet-supply shop and doggie daycare instead of a place to find a new pet.

Except for these two sweet kittens.

A Delaware rescue had taken them in and was featuring them in the store with the hope they'd get adopted quickly.

The little gray and black tabby was rambunctious and playful, and the all-black long-haired was easygoing and loved to be held and snuggled.

We played with them and loved on them for a few minutes until putting them back in the cage and heading off to our yoga class.

The next day, I couldn't stop thinking about them.

There was something about them, just like Bruno.

While I was at work, I called the pet shop and told them I'd be coming by to see the kittens.

I was considering taking the tabby when the lady working in the store came over and said, "They're brothers, you know. They were found together and haven't been separate from each other for even one second since."

While two kittens seemed like too much to handle, the black kitten looked up at me from the cage and his greenish blue eyes pierced right through my heart. I was torn between the two of them.

"If you'd like to, but are concerned about taking them both, you can always foster-to-own," the woman said. "What that means is that you can take both of them home for the weekend and see which one feels like the best fit for you. Depending on what you think you can always bring the other one back and we'll find him a home."

"Done," I said, thinking, *What's the risk?*

If it didn't work out, I'd get to spend the weekend with two sweet kittens and maybe even keep one for myself.

I filled out the paperwork for both kittens and they gave me a crate to take them home.

As I was pulling out of the pet shop parking lot in this town I'd only been to once before and have never been back to since, I looked at them through my rearview mirror and said aloud,

"You two are never going back to that place."

I had no idea how I was going to make it work with two kittens and my hectic schedule.

Plus, it was completely unlike me to make a snap decision like this. Normally I'd call both my mom and Chris, but I wanted these kittens so much I'd just made the decision on my own.

The moment I got them home I felt a wave of uncertainty that perhaps I'd made the wrong decision. I thought, *What if I can't give them a good life because I'm always on the go?*

Like I've said before, though, I worry about everything. And then I worry about the things I worry about.

In this case, I was also worried about Melky.

Melky is Chris' cat that he took in one summer while he was in college. She was nine years old at the time, and despite her sweet personality with people, she doesn't particularly like other cats. While Chris and I were living in separate cities, our plan was to hopefully move in together in the next few years.

Chris assured me, though, within just a few minutes after meeting the kittens, that we'd make it work between our three cats—and that they were, in fact, never going back to that place.

I'd asked the lady at the store before I left to connect me to the rescue. Once I was in contact with them, I asked for the contact for the person who actually rescued them so I could better understand their story and what their life was like before they came into mine.

The woman who rescued them, Siobhan, named them Oliver (the tabby) and Dodger (the long-haired) after Charles Dickens' *Oliver Twist.* She said their lives seemed to fit the story in that they were orphaned and went on a journey to find their forever home. Plus, Oliver was wild and curious and Dodger was observant and seemed to have "street smarts."

They'd been found on the side of the road in Queens, New York. They were exchanged into Siobhan's care after she saw a social media post about them and traveled to a rest stop on the New Jersey Turnpike to meet up with the lady who'd found them. From there, they made their way to Dover, Delaware with Siobhan, and once she felt they were ready for adoption, she took them to that pet-supply shop in Milton, Delaware.

Then I happened to stop by that store and decided to scoop them up and take them back to my home in Dover.

At just four months old, they'd been on quite a journey.

It took a day or two for the mutual apprehension to wear off before I was head over heels in love with these kittens.

While they were trying to get used to their new environment, their personalities showed from the first night I brought them home, and they slept—curled up together—at the foot of my bed that very first night.

My family and friends might say that I'm obsessed with them and that I've become a total cat lady. But that's ok. Because in the past two years these two orphaned kittens have become my little family.

While I've never been "alone" in life, living by yourself can be lonely. I've never felt that loneliness for one single second with these two sweet cats, who, oddly enough, both remind me so much of Bruno.

They're the perfect roommates.

Oliver and Dodger coming into my life when they did is significant because my life today looks a whole lot different than I thought it would.

It's not worse than I'd imagined, it's just different.

Growing up I had it all planned out. I was going to go to a really fancy college and cheerlead. Once I graduated I'd have an amazing, high-profile job—possibly something that would make me well-known. I'd have met the man of my dreams and we'd be married with our first of many children by the time I was 28 years old.

My mom has this saying, "Thank God I didn't get everything I thought I wanted, when I wanted it," and so many times in the past few years I've found that I can't help but to agree.

There are many things that I'm glad didn't play out exactly to my imagination, especially because I believe that things happen in the order and season in which they're supposed to happen.

Every time I'd put on my Air Force uniform with my "Boots of Abandonment," as I call them, to go to the Air Force base each day, every time I've been away for the weekend, and every time I'm separated from them for a period of time, I always come home to Oliver and Dodger, hug them both tight, and remember—that in my life today, I have everything I could ever want, it just looks different than I thought.

And it's all covered in cat hair.

# Revelation 24:

## *You get what you give.*

However much you give, more
than that will be given to you.

Take the bait,
The Universe

In middle school my mom made me pack the vacuum and cleaning supplies into the car to spend most of a day cleaning her friend's house.

I was so angry at her for making me do it, and while I tried to find a way out of it, she stuck to her guns and didn't let me slide.

We deep-cleaned the kitchen and scoured the bathrooms and dusted every surface in the house. We vacuumed the floors and Windexed all the windows and glass.

That very first time I was forced to go I complained the whole way there.

"I don't know why I have to be the one to do this," I whined to my mom in the car ride across town to their house.

"You know Kitty has MS," she said. "You know it's hard for her to do things like cleaning so I thought it would be nice to offer to clean for her."

"Yes, that's nice, but what does that have to do with me?"

While I loved Kitty and knew my mom cared deeply for her, my focus in those years was on my girlfriends, boys, and spending my weekend having fun. Not cleaning my mom's friends' houses.

Kitty's multiple sclerosis really did make it hard for her to do things like cleaning her home, but she would've never put anyone out and actually asked for the help. My mom, being the kind of person she is—and knowing that about Kitty—knew that she really could use a hand around the house.

While my mom's sobriety has a big place in my life, Kitty has so much to do with my mom getting to that place.

She was my mom's AA sponsor from the very beginning, and in so many ways, she's the person who helped my mom in her sobriety and taught her many of the lessons my mom has passed on to me.

So much of the "My mom always says..." advice I've shared over the years could easily have been interchanged with, "My mom's sponsor Kitty always says..."

I guess you could say Kitty was for my mom what my mom is for me, when it comes to the person you turn to for advice about anything and everything.

Kitty had the perfect mix of tough love and genuine understanding and relatability, and there couldn't have been a better person to walk alongside my mom in her journey through sobriety.

When my mom went to Kitty very early on and told her two people had asked my mom to sponsor them, Kitty replied by saying, "I want you to open the Big Book to the first page. What does it say?"

(That page is intentionally blank.)

"That's how much you know," she told my mom.

Tough, perhaps, but it was all from a place of love.

I have to say that I had a genuine love and appreciation for Kitty and what she meant to my mom. I was grateful for her and all the ways she'd been there to support my mom in some of the hardest years of her life.

At the same time, I still didn't get why I had to be the one cleaning her house.

That day, though, we took our time and made a day of it and made small talk with Kitty and her husband while we cleaned. Playing with her gorgeous and sweet purple-tongued Chow made up for all the work my mom made me do.

While I was mad I was forced to be there, I really did feel a sense of accomplishment after we were done.

And as we stood up from their kitchen table to leave, Kitty stood with us and hugged me tight.

With tears in her eyes she thanked me again and again and told me how hard it was for her to ask for help, but that us taking the time out of our weekend to clean her house meant so much to her and was such a big relief.

I hugged her back and told her I was happy I could help, and truly, in that very moment, I was.

We packed up the car and said our goodbyes and as we drove away from their house I looked over at my mom and said, "Kitty is so sweet and it feels really good to know that we could help her in that way, especially since she's done so much for you."

My mom said plainly, "That's why."

"That's why, what?" I asked.

"That's exactly why I made you come with me. You complained all morning about why you had to come and why you had to clean and why I was making you do this.

"It's about compassion, Sarah," she said.

"You can't buy compassion off a shelf. I can't tell you to have compassion! You have to experience true compassion for another person through giving of yourself and your time to help someone in need, expecting nothing in return."

The lesson was abundantly clear:

*You can't teach compassion, you embody it by helping others and expecting nothing in return.*

And again there's Soc in my head, *Service to others. There's no higher purpose.*

From that day on, I was happy to clean Kitty's house, and actually, I looked forward to the opportunity.

Throughout my life I've been surrounded by givers. People who give of themselves time and time again for the simple fact that they love to.

The kind of people who give because it's inherent in their being.

My parents call them "salt of the earth" kinds of people.

And I've been blessed to know so many.

I've learned over the years that giving to others comes in many forms. Whether it's your time, your money, your resources, energy, or expertise, there's no wrong way to give.

Life for me today is less about what I can get but rather, what I can give.

And I've found that when your intentions are pure and your heart is in the right place, every time you give of yourself to others it comes right back to you in an even bigger way.

In thinking back to the lesson I learned from Kitty all those years ago, I think it's important to correct my own lesson:

It's not *just* that you get what you give.

As my mom, and Kitty, and so many other givers have taught me: more accurately, you always get back—tenfold—what you give.

# Revelation 25:

## *The hardest decision you'll ever have to make is the one that's best for you.*

Sometimes, when circumstances or disappointments
bump you off track, it's the beginning of an even bigger
dream coming true, that could not have come true on the
track you were on. Yeah, always.

Always, always,
The Universe

I used to think that there was this loud, overt *knowing* about making life decisions—like what career path to take, or whether or not he's "the one."

I thought that in these moments, it's as if the heavens opened up and the answer was revealed to us like it was written plainly in the sky.

But life is just not that way.

In October 2016 I got on the phone with the assignments manager to talk about options for my next job as an Air Force public affairs officer.

I added my top three choices, in order, for Washington D.C., New York City, or Los Angeles to what we call in the Air Force our career "dream sheet."

My thinking was that if I could finish out my active duty career at the Pentagon, it would set me up for great opportunities to run my health coaching business in D.C. once I separated. I picked NYC and LA for those same reasons—a big city in which to launch my entrepreneurial career.

Again, my mindset was to plan as if I was going to be in the Air Force for the long haul, and also like I'd be ready to get out tomorrow.

It was sounding absolutely positive that I was going to get the Pentagon job. In fact, the assignments manager told me it was 99.9 percent likely.

I should say, though, I didn't actually want another assignment. What I really wanted was to get out of the military and take my business full time. But as long as I had the safety net to fall back on, my business was just an *if it works out* kind of thing.

But in February 2017, just four months before I was expecting to move, I was told there was absolutely no way—zero chance, is what that same assignments manager told me—that I could get any of those three locations.

Instead, I was offered a job to work with NATO for two years at the Allied Joint Force Command in the Netherlands.

In other words, a better job. I was offered a dream job.

Except, for me, it wasn't *my* dream.

If you'd asked me four or five years prior, I would have absolutely said yes. Wouldn't have even had a second thought about it.

But the way I saw it now was that it was forcing me to put my life on hold.

I never dreamed about working for NATO, but for the past four years I'd thought almost all day, every single day, about running a successful health coaching business and creating my life on my terms.

I thought to myself, *What about my dream sheet?*

Not the one for the Air Force, but the dream sheet for my life.

And what I quickly learned is that there never was—and is never going to be—a perfect time to do anything in life, even if, as I mentioned previously, I was prepared and ready.

Now when I got the call, I was working a short-term assignment at MacDill Air Force Base in Tampa, Florida. I'd been sent there from my home station in Delaware for six months.

It was a job I was completely unqualified for but was grateful for the chance to lead and for the opportunity to learn so much.

That job reaffirmed for me that I'm capable of more than I ever give myself credit for.

I felt confident that I could stay in the military and make a good life of it. But the appeal of running a business and the chance to chase a dream was something I'd been working towards for several years by getting the education, acquiring certifications, running a website, blogging, and creating programs to help others improve their health and their lives.

So when the offer to move to Europe landed in my lap, I asked for a day to think it over.

I went home that night and researched everything I could about the base, the area, the nearest cities, airports, train stations, and everything you could possibly think of to do. I looked at apartments, gyms, restaurants, and coffee shops, and I tried to imagine what my life could be like living in Europe and working for NATO.

I'd be almost 32 years old before I'd have the chance to separate again.

I thought about what would happen to my relationship, the moments I'd miss with family and friends, and the fact that I'd be putting my business on hold.

At the same time, I felt like it was crazy not to take the job.

*What if I don't take it and it ends up being one of the biggest regrets of my life?* I thought.

Here's how I made the decision.

After spending time visualizing, weighing the pros and cons, and talking with the select group of people whose opinions really matter to me, I chose.

That's the thing about making decisions.

The Latin word, "decision" literally translates to "to cut off."

Making a decision is to cut off other courses of action.

I gave myself one day to think about it because I didn't want to obsess about the options and then be guilted into a choice as a result of overthinking.

My mom taught me at a very early age that when I was struggling with a decision or with what to say to someone, wait 24 hours and then see how I felt.

That advice in mind, I went to bed that night and had the most peaceful and restful sleep.

In the morning, I called the assignments manager and politely declined the assignment.

Additionally, I informed him that I'd be separating from active duty upon not taking the assignment.

I remembered something my mom always told me, "The hardest decision you'll ever have to make is the one that's best for you."

That was an understatement in this case.

But I'd decided.

I'll never forget what Chris and I talked about on the phone the night I was weighing my options.

He said plainly, "Sarah, if you really want this assignment, then take it. I will support you 100 percent and you and I will be just fine."

He's always selfless and supportive in that way.

But he couldn't come with me because we would've had to have been married. Also, in the time that I'd been working in Florida, he'd left his job in D.C. for a new position in Philadelphia.

His career was gaining a lot of momentum, and I respected that he wouldn't want to leave to follow me to Europe.

"The thing is," he continued, "You're going to have to give me a better reason than, 'I just want to live in Europe and travel on the weekends,' as your reason for actually taking this job, because for the past four years you've talked about nothing but wanting to get out of the military and run your business. I thought that was your dream."

You can see clearly why I love him so much.

He's straight with no chaser.

And I took to heart what he said.

The job in the Netherlands was appealing because of my passion for travel, but could I really put my business off any longer?

I'd given almost 10 years of my life to the Air Force, including the time I spent in ROTC.

And more than I was afraid of failing as an entrepreneur, I was afraid that if I stayed for another assignment, that the fire I had to chase my dreams would burn out.

The thing is, just because you make a difficult decision—even if it's the best decision for you—doesn't mean that your life will get any easier or that things will simply fall into place.

In fact, for me, things got harder.

When I returned to Delaware from my assignment in Florida, I began the separation process from active duty.

I went to one meeting and appointment after another, and as I signed document after document, taking away my comfortable life and safety net one signature at a time, I began to panic.

*What if I don't have what it takes?*

*What if this doesn't work out?*

*What if everyone who doesn't believe in me is actually right?*

*What if I'm not capable?*

*What if I spend my whole life hustling just to get by?*

*What if I was supposed to take that job?*

At the time, I wasn't making a whole lot of money in my business and I didn't have the clientele I needed to pay all the bills.

Chris reminded me by asking me again,

"What's the worst that could happen?"

Thankfully, he repeats this for me often because apparently it still hasn't fully sunken in.

Again, he's quite loveable.

So I took his advice, and during this transition period, I made note of all the things I knew for sure about myself and I took stock of what I had available to me.

Part of taking stock included a list—what has become the 29 lessons in this book.

And writing that list of what I've learned along the way made me realize that I couldn't put off writing this book any longer and that I couldn't miss my goal to publish before turning 30 years old.

So I wrote it from April until August 2017 while I was on my terminal leave and working through the separation process.

I had several months worth of leave that I'd saved up, meaning I was getting paid my full salary, housing, and benefits as I navigated the transition period, and spent most of my time at home working on this book and my business.

The first few weeks were incredible—*This is what it's like to be your own boss, work from anywhere, and never have to dread a Monday ever again!*—I thought.

But soon after I fell into a horrible depression.

It wasn't just that my career was changing, it was that my whole life was changing all at once.

I was making all of these big plans for my future, including a move to a new city, building a business, and taking on a completely new responsibility as an Air Force Reservist.

For the past decade, my life was very well regimented by the military, and now—while it was what I wanted—my success is totally up to me.

The weight of it all finally came to a head and the overwhelm was hard to shake.

It took me moving through those weeks and all the fear and feelings I was having about everything changing to finally find my footing and feel confident in picking myself up and moving forward.

I'd secured a Reserve job at Dover Air Force Base through the network of people I'd spent the past three years working with.

Because the plan was to move back to Philadelphia to finally live in the same city as Chris (after three years of living in different cities), it meant having to drive only 90 minutes one weekend per month back to Delaware for drill duty.

It ended up being the perfect way to transition to civilian life, and has helped me not to worry so much about the immediate success of my business.

So most recently, I've learned that the hardest decision you'll ever have to make, is the one that's *best* for you.

But that doesn't mean you shouldn't make it.

In the Air Force Reserve, there are opportunities to serve all over the world all the time. I now have the opportunity to serve my monthly weekend drill duty or to volunteer to go on orders anywhere in the world.

I have a pretty good feeling I'll get to work with NATO in the Netherlands, after all.

# Revelation 26:

## *It's definitely about the journey.*

Nobody is who they are based upon one decision, one day,
one path, one chance, one relationship, or one anything else.
Every day is brand new and opportunity never stops knocking.

Who's there?
The Universe

"The journey," Dan said. "It's the journey that brings us happiness, not the destination."

We're back to the movie "Peaceful Warrior," where Socrates tells Dan he's ready for him to see the "thing" he's been wanting to show him.

They go on a hike, and after three hours of walking up a mountain Dan starts getting impatient and asking when they're going to get to whatever the big "thing" is that Soc is supposed to show him.

Soc stops and says, "We're here."

Confused, Dan looks around and wonders what he could be talking about. Was it the view? Was it the flower in the grass at their feet? The rock in the grass next to the flower?

Dan is noticeably upset that there's not some big surprise to be had at the climax of this hike.

Soc reminds Dan that he was excited the entire time they were on the hike.

Then he admits that he wasn't actually sure what they'd find...that he never is.

This is when Dan realizes the lesson.

"It's the journey that brings us happiness, not the destination," he yells, after Soc has already begun hiking back down the mountain.

I could totally relate to Dan.

For me, it took some time for the hurt and embarrassment to wear off before I could believe that for myself.

When I set out to compete in my first figure competition, I wanted to win.

Who wouldn't?

You don't dedicate nine months of your life—as I had—to training every single day (sometimes twice a day) and giving everything you have not to want to win.

Then on the night of the competition as I'm standing on stage next to the other girls and in front of my parents and friends, the judges called the third-place winner.

It wasn't me.

So now I was in the running for second or first.

They called the second-place winner.

I had to have won.

They called the first-place winner.

And suddenly I hadn't even placed in the top three.

I was embarrassed that my parents flew all the way to Guam to be there to support me in my competition.

I felt stupid that all my friends paid money and showed up that night to watch me on stage.

I was reluctant to share on social media that I hadn't won after spending nine months posting about my training and transformation and progress towards that one night—that single moment on that stage.

It wasn't until I had some time and space from not winning to realize how much I had to be grateful for on the journey that led me to that stage—how much I'd actually won.

Just 10 months prior, as I told you before, I'd decided I was sick and tired of being sick and tired and not treating my body well.

I didn't want to have an eating disorder anymore, but in all those years I suffered I just never learned a better way.

So in 2013 I decided to create one for myself.

In addition to that fitness transformation photo I saw on Instagram of that one girl, I'd also had a dream in that time that I was standing on a stage in an emerald green bikini with lights shining in my face. I could see my body in my dream, and I was fit, toned, and tanned just like the girl in the photo.

That's when I decided that I was going to pursue whatever that *thing* was.

At the time, I knew absolutely nothing about bodybuilding. I'd never even heard of figure competitions and I had no clue it was this massive thing that millions of people are part of...that it's actually considered a sport. I was ignorant to that entire world.

I didn't know how to train for a competition, what it took to do it, how you should go about getting started, or how I was going to get there. I just knew that I was going to do it.

It was exactly the same way I'd felt when I decided to join the military.

So I emailed Chris while I was visiting my family for the holidays and asked him if he would help me with working out when I got back to Guam. He was the one person I knew on the island who was always in the gym, always working out, always eating healthy, and seemed to be really committed to his health and fitness.

He wasn't a personal trainer, had no knowledge or experience in bodybuilding, but was passionate about his own health and said he'd help where he could.

That was all I needed—someone who could help me figure it out.

And that's how the journey began. We dove in head first and worked our butts off to learn as much as we possibly could. We identified all the things we needed to learn and then split up the tasks. Along the way I blogged about the experience and we did weekly YouTube video recaps of my training and progress.

A few months into the training I had thousands of people following along and received tons of encouragement and well wishes. I was finding that I also received loads of questions.

From people I'd gone to high school or college with, to total strangers who saw my blog or videos and decided to follow my story, people told me they felt inspired by my journey and also wanted to know how to create those same positive changes in their lives.

At the time, I was also in the middle of considering which school to do my master's degree in public relations at online.

Like my days at Temple when I switched from biophysics to journalism and political science, I took a sharp right turn and decided to try exercise science instead.

Three months into my training I began my master's degree at California University of Pennsylvania online, and a year later I graduated with a master's degree in exercise science with a concentration in wellness and fitness.

Simultaneously, I earned certifications as both a personal trainer and nutrition specialist, and then went on to become a life coach as well.

Giving up my disordered eating habits to become a true athlete was, looking back, a decision that has changed the trajectory of my life.

I've learned now that it wasn't so much that *I* was sick or disordered, but my habits and mindset were, and it was only because I didn't think I knew how to do it better or different.

Little did I know back then that working on healing myself and sharing my experiences would motivate and inspire others.

I simply started sharing my story online as an accountability mechanism for me, and so my family and friends could keep up with my training since I lived halfway around the world.

Little did I know that would then inspire me to pursue the path of entrepreneurship and creating a living by helping others improve their health based on the solid foundation of my education and the way I'd taught myself.

I witnessed in myself during those months of training strength I never knew I had.

I was up every day at 4 a.m. before work to be in the gym for several hours before going to the office, then oftentimes doing another workout at lunch or in the evening.

On the weekends I was always up early doing research or studying, posing and working out at the gym, and in the grocery store and kitchen getting my meals prepared for the week ahead.

Every day I went to work, studied my butt off for school in the three master's classes I was taking at a time, and made enough time to get the eight-to-nine hours of sleep my training required.

It was a brutal schedule, especially as a new public affairs officer trying to learn my job, lead a team of people, and work directly for a general officer.

Every time I got up to that alarm, every time I completed a workout or a meal, with each blog post and video, after every posing practice, day after day, I realized that not only did I have what it takes to stand up on that stage proudly—given all my effort to get there—but that I'd had the strength to do all of those things the same way I've been able to work through every other obstacle or challenge in my life.

Those nine months of training became proof for me that I'm endlessly capable of more.

The one thing not winning that competition reaffirmed for me—like it did for Dan on that mountain—is that it's definitely about the journey.

If it had only been about winning, this would be an unfortunate story.

But along that journey I discovered my personal path to freedom from the disordered way of living that I'd suffered from for more than a decade.

I pursued what was now just the beginning of my educational path to learning everything I could ever want to know about health, wellness, exercise, and nutrition, and in the past five years I've impacted hundreds of others and helped people improve their health, physique, their body image, and their lives.

Yeah, it's definitely about the journey.

Thanks, Soc.

# Revelation 27:

## *The greater the struggle,*
## *the more glorious the triumph.*

It's not that your life totally rocks, except for a few tricky
spots, slippery patches, and challenges. But that your
life totally rocks, in large part, because of the tricky
spots, slippery patches, and challenges.

Stranger than fiction,
The Universe


In the short film, "The Butterfly Circus," we're introduced to a showman and his team of performers of a small circus act at the height of the Great Depression. The showman discovers a limbless man, played by Nick Vujicic, being exploited at a carnival sideshow. The man finds a way to escape the carnival, joins the Butterfly Circus, and learns he can achieve more than he ever thought was possible.

For the sake of this chapter's lesson, I'm going to have to go ahead and spoil some parts of the film.

The performers pass through a tiny desert community and wow the people with wonder. As they perform, the limbless man waits by the cars, watching the performers move with strength, color, and grace, as the showman describes them.

"But if you could only see the beauty that comes from ashes," the showman says to the limbless man.

The film takes us back through the performers' lives and shows us how each of them struggled before getting to the circus.

"But they're different than me," the limbless man says.

"Yes. You do have an advantage," the showman says.

"The greater the struggle, the more glorious the triumph."

I spent a lot of time in the years following losing our house wondering why my family had to go through such hardship. *What's the point of all this struggle?* I always wondered.

I've come to learn in the years since, that the showman's words are true: *The greater the struggle, the more glorious the triumph.*

Those hard years made it possible for me to be where I am today.

I couldn't have known this then, but every struggle, every sacrifice, every grueling and exhausting day and every tear-filled, sleepless night would all prove to be worth it to stand here on the other side of it all, having overcome so many obstacles and persisting, in spite of every time it felt like I just couldn't carry on for one more day.

Here's the thing. Bad things happen to good people every day. I've met people whose situations were much worse than mine had ever been. But we all struggle in our own ways—we each have to fight our own battles.

It's said that hindsight is 20/20 and that's been absolutely true for me. Looking back on my life, I am eternally grateful for what happened to my family and for each moment that brought me to this point.

I love the phrase by Marie Forleo that, "Everything is figureoutable."

In my case it was, just as it is for you, too.

Was my life up to now as hard as some people have it? Will it ever be any harder down the road?

I don't think either of those things are the point.

The Butterfly Circus performers later pull over to a river where everyone is swimming, bathing, and enjoying themselves.

The limbless man ends up at the riverbank on a rock next to a log that he's trying to cross to get to the rest of the group. He calls out to them, only to find that they're ignoring him—perhaps they can't hear him.

So he takes it upon himself to try and cross the log on his own, and as he does, he falls into the river.

When the performers notice he's nowhere to be found, they all begin yelling out and calling for him and running to the place they last saw him.

Just as they cross the river, the limbless man surfaces from beneath the water, smiling, laughing, and cheering, as he's discovered that he can swim on his own.

The limbless man's circus act becomes standing on a high-dive platform and launching himself off into a tiny pool of water below, showing the audience he can swim even without arms or legs.

For all the drowning and flailing I feel like I've done, along the way I've learned how to swim.

And my life today, after being broken down to nothing—like the Marines—and building it all back up, is a glorious triumph.

It doesn't mean that life may never be hard again or that I'm invincible and will never struggle. Rather, I'm now ready—and better prepared—to deal with the things life throws at us.

I'm not broken, nothing's ruined, and as I promised myself all those years ago, I'm not jaded.

Instead, I look at life as if every day is a choice.

If I'm lucky enough to open my eyes to a brand-new day, it means the choice is mine to live in the moment or spend it preoccupied with things I can't change. I can choose happiness, or be a victim. I can help others, or selfishly fend for myself. I can keep dreaming or give up hope.

The former of each of those scenarios is not always the easier choice. But each has proved, in very profound ways, to be worth it.

Today, when things get hard or life takes a wrong turn, I try to remember how much I've overcome and I try to remember that—like the showman says—I do have an advantage:

The greater the struggle, the more glorious the triumph.

# Revelation 28:

## *You control what happens next.*

Life is a chance to do things your way; not the cheapest way,
not the most popular way, and not how others think you
should. And a very, very, very precious chance, at that.

Got Chills?
The Universe

He always seemed angry. But it took almost a year for me to really understand why.

Chris joined Air Force ROTC at the University of Central Florida, like me, because he didn't really see another way. He needed the money, and working two side jobs writing for the school paper and folding clothes at American Eagle wasn't cutting it.

Billy, his brother, was diagnosed in August 2006. Pancreatic cancer is rare for a person that age. He was 24 years old and the prognosis from early on wasn't good.

Anyone who joins the military does so knowing that they don't control where they are stationed. It's part of service. But Chris made it a goal to succeed early in his career so that he had some say in his future assignments, as he hoped to get stationed relatively close to Florida, where Billy and his parents lived.

When Chris commissioned on May 6, 2007, he moved to Pope Air Force Base in North Carolina for his first assignment.

From Pope, he was then sent to South Korea for a year.

Following that assignment, he was stationed at Charleston Air Force Base in South Carolina.

Shortly after getting there he was sent on a deployment for seven months.

Just after he returned from that deployment he spent six weeks in Alabama for training.

While in Alabama, he was told that when he returned to Charleston, he'd have three days to pack up his apartment and move on to another deployment, which ended up lasting eight months.

So finally, once he was back in Charleston, he expected to be off the hook for another deployment for some time.

But three months after finishing that second deployment, he was called into his boss' office and told he could either take another deployment, which would last about 13 months, or he could spend two years stationed on Guam.

Full of resentment for the Air Force and angry with his boss, who couldn't do more to help keep him closer to his brother— let alone to keep him stateside—Chris took the assignment to Guam.

He packed his things for another move overseas and his sixth duty assignment in six years.

He chose Guam, because unlike the deployment, he'd at least be able to leave to make the 26-hour flight home to Billy if or when needed.

Eleven months into his assignment on Guam, he was tagged with another deployment, this time, for six months.

Upon returning to Guam in anticipation of another assignment, Chris pushed hard to be stationed in Tampa, Florida—a 40-minute drive from where Billy lived.

His brother's condition had worsened since his time being stationed on Guam, and he'd made that 26-hour journey home more than once to see Billy in the two years he lived halfway around the world.

The day the assignments dropped, so did Chris' faith in the Air Force. He'd been assigned to the Pentagon instead, and while he was grateful to be going to a large city where he'd be able to easily get on a flight to Tampa, his resentment grew stronger from all the times he'd stepped up, sacrificed, and served so far away from his sick brother, and then still not being able to catch a break.

Chris got the call on May 8, 2014. Billy had gone into seizures the evening prior and was unresponsive. Chris was still on Guam and was set to move to Washington D.C. in July.

The Air Force put him on a Red Cross emergency flight to Florida to rush to his brother's side, but Billy had already passed before he'd even made it home. He spent several days in Florida with his mom and dad, arranging his brother's funeral and packing up all of Billy's things.

In the eight years Chris served, he saw Billy less than 20 times. The closest he'd ever been stationed was 434 miles away. But even through the distance, they'd grown closer in those years they were apart. They texted and emailed back and forth each day and Chris traveled home to see Billy whenever he could.

The way the regulations work, the service considers your parents, spouse, and children your "family." But outside of that, siblings—sometimes the only family a person has—are not enough to qualify for an exception to a specific assignment or for not taking a deployment.

Back when Chris was stationed at Pope, he was put in charge of his office for several months while his boss was deployed. As a young lieutenant, he was sharp and noticeably good at his job, but was also noticeably angry—the same way I'd noticed it when I'd met him and worked with him on Guam.

So when one of the public affairs leaders from headquarters came to visit the base and Chris' office, he and this other officer got along well and Chris was able to confide in him about all the things he had going on at 22 years old, and the frustrations he was feeling.

The morning the colonel left, he'd left a note on Chris' desk. It encouraged him to keep his head up and applauded him for doing an incredible job—that people were noticing his hard work and effort.

Not thinking he'd see him again that day, Chris was surprised when he ran into the colonel just as he was leaving. Chris thanked him for the note as he walked him to his car, when the colonel turned to him and said, "If there's one thing I know, you have the ability to make decisions."

He continued, "If you forget that, you always need to remember that you control what happens next." He wrote that phrase down, "You control what happens next" on a small piece of paper, folded it up, and handed it over to Chris.

Chris kept that paper in his uniform pocket until it was worn and no longer readable, and continues living by that motto as his personal mantra for life.

Fast forward five years from that time and here was Chris, handing across his desk to me a pink sticky note. On it, he'd written, "You control what happens next."

That sticky stayed in my uniform pocket until it was so worn I placed it in a Ziploc bag and hung it on my fridge.

Ultimately, Chris separated from the Air Force after spending just over a year at the Pentagon.

He doesn't hold those resentments for the Air Force anymore—that's the sacrifice you make when you volunteer to serve. But going off that colonel's advice, Chris had the ability to control what happened next for him, and ultimately that was a life and a career that didn't include moving every two-to-three years with the uncertainty of a deployment always looming in the future.

I had a chance to meet Billy in 2012 when I was home from Guam visiting my family for Christmas. He met me at the Tampa airport when I was picking up a friend so that he could give me Chris' Christmas gifts to take back to Guam with me. We met in the cell phone waiting lot and he was dressed in a suit that had become at least four or five sizes too big for him because of how much weight he'd lost. I asked him why he was dressed up and he said it was, "Just because."

So when I look at that pink sticky note, the paper worn and fuzzy with a permanent crease in the middle, I picture Billy standing at the trunk of his car in his baggy suit, handing me the Christmas gifts for his younger brother, who was Billy's biggest supporter.

It was the first time I felt like I understood Chris, and that allowed our friendship to grow stronger.

He wasn't angry, but he carried with him—like that note in his pocket—the weight of his family.

And sometimes, the love of our family is the heaviest burden to bear.

Like me, and like Chris, we all have a story.

Life's been messy at times for all of us.

So I think it's less about what happens to you than it is about what you choose to do about it.

If Chris were writing a chapter of this book or was able to give you one piece of advice, I'm pretty confident it would be this:

*You control what happens next.*

# Revelation 29:

## *Such is Life.*

You know how everyone is always talking about life
being a journey, not a destination? And that it's the journey
that really counts? That from it, you'll find your purpose,
meaning, and true happiness? Well, this is it.

Soak it in,
The Universe

In the years that followed losing our home my parents remained quite close. My dad stopped by each day to help my mom with her business and would frequently be at the house for dinner and to see whichever of us kids was in town at any given time.

Looking back, it seems insane and hard to fathom how it all happened the way it did and how we managed to function as a family in those years.

In October 2012, my mom decided to move to Florida. It wasn't an easy decision to leave but it was necessary in order to move forward. As was normal, my mom elicited help from my dad and they made the drive from Pennsylvania to Florida with only the things that sat in storage left over from our old house and our one dog, Baby.

Both sides of my extended family live in Florida. This was a perfect move for my mom to be closer to her mom and siblings.

Now my grandma would have five of her six children with her in Florida.

My uncle helped her pick out a small villa in Wesley Chapel that she'd rent and go from there.

For several years she'd been running her own business making what are called reborn dolls.

Essentially, they're life-size newborn dolls, the parts made by sculptors, and my mom hand-paints every single detail onto the doll, assembles them, roots each piece of hair one by one, and by the time she's done, these dolls look exactly like a real baby.

You'd never know—until you reached out and touched them—that they're just dolls. She sells them on eBay all over the world and has sold more than a thousand dolls over the years.

At the same time, my dad had a relatively new job in Arizona working in nuclear power, the same field he worked in decades before when my parents were first married.

So the money from my dad's job and my mom's business was enough for my mom to start over in a new place.

Like the phone call where my whole world fell apart, I never expected the call I got from my mom while on Guam and the casual tone of her voice.

"So your dad helped me get all settled and moved in to the new house."

*That was really cool of my dad,* I thought.

"I told him that this is his home, too," she said. "So if he wants a place to stay when he's not on contract in Arizona, this is the place he can come home to."

*Huh?*

After the foreclosure, I moved 15 different times in the five years I spent in college before leaving for my first Air Force assignment on Guam.

Each semester I had a new bedroom in a new house in a new part of Philadelphia.

I'd had five different jobs, and two internships; the one at FOX 29 News, and another working in the Mayor of Philadelphia's communications office, giving me a first-hand look at what it's actually like to be the mayor—like I'd wanted—and getting to "speak to the city" through crafting his public remarks and press releases.

I studied abroad in Rome, earned a full ride for college, and graduated with a bachelor's degree in two disciplines and a commission as a second lieutenant in the United States Air Force.

I looked out the window of my condo, at the tiny island in the aqua blue water, just off the shore from the beach.

*How did we get here?* I thought.

Since getting stationed on Guam, I've traveled the world, spent six-and-a-half years on active duty as a public affairs officer, earned my master's degree, became a personal trainer, nutrition specialist, and life coach.

I've paid off all my debt, put money in the bank, and started a business, following my dream of being an entrepreneur.

You're reading this very book because I reached my goal of becoming a published author before turning 30 years old.

There's a quote I learned back in college that goes like this:

"If this year has taught me anything, it is that you should go with the flow, take chances, and be spontaneous. Party until the sun comes up, push the envelope, and dare to dream. Best friends are the only way to keep you sane and allow you to go crazy all at the same time. The pieces eventually fall into place. Until then, laugh at the confusion and live for the moment. Life is too short to wake up in the morning with regrets. So, love the people who treat you right, forget about the ones who don't, and believe that everything happens for a reason. If you get a chance, take it. If it changes your life, let it. Nobody said it would be easy. They just promised that it would be worth it."

As I've learned, the pieces do eventually fall into place.

Today, my oldest brother, Josh, is happily married to the love of his life. They live in Washington D.C. and he absolutely adores his teaching job.

Mitchell is married to his high school sweetheart. They stayed together even through the distance the Marine Corps put between them. He served proudly for four years and lives in his beautiful home in Allentown. The Marine Corps paid for that college education that was a waste of his time and my parents' money all those years ago. He applies the work ethic he learned in the Marine Corps not just to his current career, but in every area of his life.

Jaclyn's passion for travel was ignited in the months we spent in Rome and on Guam and continues today. She's a security forces officer in the Air Force and was promoted to captain in 2016. She's served so far in Ohio and North Dakota. Jax also earned a full scholarship that paid for her criminal justice degree at Temple. She's earned and paid for her master's degree, and while we struggled to afford a piece of pizza and a glass of wine in Rome, today she's proud not to have any debt to her name, either.

My mom and dad are happily married.

*Wait, when did that happen?* You might be wondering.

Perhaps ironically, they were too broke to ever get an official divorce all those years ago. And after those years of separation and hardship, their relationship is better today than it ever has been.

My dad spent several years unemployed after being let go from his job but has a position today that has helped my parents pay off their debts and live comfortably.

They live in a gorgeous home in Wesley Chapel that has a room for each of us kids to come and stay during the holidays.

Our Christmases today are not without gifts.

For my family, eventually the pieces all fell into place.

I mentioned early on that not all blessings come in good things, and oftentimes the blessing isn't revealed to us for quite some time.

And what I wrote to my family on the back of that picture frame all those years ago couldn't be more true today.

"You never see the hard times in the photographs, but they are what get you from one happy snapshot to the next. Wherever the road ahead may take you, remember always where it was you came from."

My family has been down a long and winding road. But like Miss Kathy taught me, God never gives us more than we can handle.

It's like all of her constant prayers for my family all those years ago have been and were being answered all along.

Today, we're a stronger family than ever before, and our lives—individually—are immensely better than any of us could've ever imagined.

Who knows if things will always be this way, as I've found that life is rarely ever predictable.

As my mom always says,

Such is life.

# A Final Note

The idea of turning 30 years old has always felt like a big deal to me. I joked that in your early 20s turning 30 seems like forever away, but I genuinely believed back then that 30 was so far in the future—and I could never picture my life today all those years ago.

If the speed of the past decade is any indication of how quickly life passes by, I can only hope that my 30s are filled with the kinds of people and experiences that my teens and twenties were.

As I move forward with my business and my Air Force Reserve career, I'm walking into this next chapter of my life feeling both humbled and grateful.

I was given the gift of desperation early in life. A gift, because without all the hard stuff, I'm not so sure I'd be where I am today. When I felt lost, or when I was broke, or when I felt like there was no hope…there's always been someone put in my path to remind me that life is so good.

Writing this book has been a transformative experience. Each of these lessons had their place and meaning during the time that I lived them, but I've relived all these memories as if they happened just yesterday.

I feel as though I've healed old wounds and found closure. As I said in the very beginning—this has been cleansing for my soul.

I've also reconnected with many of the people who've impacted my life in such significant ways—many of the people whose stories you read in these pages.

To be able to reach out, thank them, and tell each of these amazing human beings how their presence in my life matters, makes me feel as though I'm the luckiest girl in the world.

One place I felt I lacked closure was with Miss Kathy. So in finally sitting down to tell the story about how she opened up her home and her heart to me and took care of me when there was a lot on the line, I became more determined than ever to find her. I solicited the help of my dad, and after brainstorming options, we started by searching for Philadelphia housing records.

For whatever reason, it'd been so hard to figure out how to find Miss Kathy and her brother before without knowing their full names. But this time around, it took a matter of a few minutes.

Once we found several names from housing records I immediately got on Facebook and started running searches. I first found Miss Kathy's brother, Jimmy, and through a quick search of his friends I found her. There she was, right there on Facebook, her sparkling brown eyes and that smile that always cheered me up.

*I finally found her.*

I was so excited I didn't know what to do first. I was shaking, and my mind was racing at the thought of how to see her, the possibility that I could actually wrap my arms around her and hug her, and that I could finally thank her for all she'd done for me.

*Do I send her a message?*

*Should I wait until I know what I want to say?*

And after reading the first post on her Facebook wall, my heart shattered.

Miss Kathy had passed away on October 8, 2016 in her home in Texas.

I found out this tragic news on the day that I was shooting my cover and author photos for this book, and while I wanted to cancel and hide in bed under the covers, I pictured Miss Kathy in her run-down apartment, thanking Jesus for her home and her mop and her buckets and the rain...and, again, that God never gives us more than we can handle.

I mentioned that I always felt like Miss Kathy was an angel, as if she came into my life when I most needed it, and went on her way when it was time for me to move forward with my life.

She's been my very own Soc, like Socrates taught Dan to be a peaceful warrior.

And though she's gone, I have a strong feeling—as with Jason—that she hasn't actually left.

So I've been saying all the things I've wanted to say to her over the years...and I'm confident that she hears me.

*There are no coincidences.*

My mom's recommendation all those years ago was to write a book about my life experiences and the things I'd been through so that girls my age who may be struggling wouldn't have to feel alone.

Please share this book with a young lady in your life. You never know how it might change her world, like all of the AA meetings, inspirational websites, quote books and calendars, and self-help books that have helped me over the years.

Perhaps it will inspire young girls around the world, as was the intention all those years ago.

Or perhaps it has inspired *you.*

If so, maybe after the final page—after you close this book— you'll remember to take life *One day at a time.* Or maybe you'll ask yourself, *Why not you?* Perhaps you'll be reminded that *Miracles happen every single day.*

Maybe you'll agree that *There's no higher purpose than service* and that *You get what you give.* If *Life's hard,* maybe you'll *Pray harder.* Or maybe you *Don't take yourself so seriously* from here.

No matter which of these resonates most with you, my hope is that you remember this:

*It's definitely about the journey.*

---

In Memory of Candice Adams Ismirle:
Donations for the children of fallen Airmen can be made to the Red River Valley Fighter Pilots Association on their website at www.river-rats.org. Click the "Give Direct" button, and if you'd like for your donation to go to Rafe and Ryder, specifically, in the comments block enter: "In memory of Candice Ismirle."


Support One Leg Up On Life:
To support Christy and Jessica Wise as they continue to provide prosthetic limbs to children who cannot afford them, visit their website at www.oneleguponlife.org and click the "Donate/Volunteer" button to make monetary donations, volunteer your time, or submit continued prayers for the Foundation.

---

Don't forget your free printable!
Head to sarahbergstein.com/book to get your hands on your
very own free *Such is Life* "29 Revelations" printable that you
can hang in a special place for ongoing motivation and
inspiration!

# Acknowledgements

Self-publishing is not a solo effort. In fact, this book would be nothing without the people who've helped to ensure this life goal of mine was accomplished, and on time, at that.

To Chris, my number one fan, biggest supporter, editor, coach, therapist, chauffer, chief of book operations, cheerleader, partner in crime—*my person*. Thank you for encouraging me, for your thorough editing and loving feedback, for listening and providing sage advice, and for helping to make this project so much fun along the way. Thank you for your support with this book and in absolutely everything I do. Thank you for believing in me. ILYTSM!

To my mom, Sharon, who encouraged me to see this goal through when I thought maybe I should just let it slide. Thank you, mom, for pushing me to achieve this goal, and all of my biggest dreams. You've always been my hero. I love you more. Shoulders up!

To my dad, Sandy, who listened while I read draft chapters aloud and boosted my confidence in my writing. Thank you, dad, for always being there for me no matter what, in everything I've ever done in life. In the way of dads, you're the very best there is. I love you—your "Unforgettable."

To Bernie Kale and Damien Taylor, thank you, gents. You two made this project fun and full of laughter. Thank you for helping to bring this dream to life and for taking the visions in my head and making them a reality that people can hold in their hands.

To my closest girlfriends, who rallied behind me and held a number of roles in supporting this project along the way. Thanks for always listening and being there. I'm so lucky to call each of you a friend and love you all to pieces.

To my entire Launch Squad, your desire to support and care for this project has been overwhelming. There are 29 lessons in this book but I learned another one from all of you—there are so many loving people who care, and who are happy to support. Don't overlook those people. I'm sure glad I didn't—thank you all from the bottom of my very full heart.

Each person mentioned in this book has played an extremely important role in my life. I said earlier in the book that I've sometimes felt late to the game in life. Or that I've wondered if maybe I was exactly on time. There are countless people who've been put in my path, in addition to those mentioned here, who make me feel like I am and always have been exactly right where I need to be, and surround by exactly the right people.

My life is so good I feel like I'm cheating.

# About the Author

Sarah Bergstein is the author of *Such is Life: 29 Life Revelations from a 30-Year-Old Dreamer*, which was released on October 16, 2017—the date of Sarah's 30th birthday—following a goal she'd set in her early 20s to be a published author before turning 30 years old.

Released in 2017, Sarah's first book shares her stories of love and loss, success and failure, overcoming obstacles, chasing dreams, and finding hope along the way. The 29 revelations, or lessons, are told through the stories of her experiences, and from the lives of people she's met and been moved by along the way.

Sarah is an officer in the Air Force Reserve after spending six and a half years serving as an active duty Air Force public affairs director in Guam, Delaware, and Florida. She's pursued her dreams of being an entrepreneur and runs an online health coaching business serving busy female entrepreneurs, professionals, and leaders around the world, to help women master their health so they can live their best, healthiest lives.

Learn more by visiting her site at sarahbergstein.com or by connecting with Sarah on Facebook (facebook.com/sarahbergstein), Instagram (@sarahbergstein), or Twitter (@sarah_bergstein).